TOOLS FOR COMMUNITY PARTICIPATION

A MANUAL FOR
TRAINING TRAINERS IN PARTICIPATORY TECHNIQUES

Lyra Srinivasan

PROWWESS/UNDP Technical Series
Involving Women in Water and Sanitation

LESSONS STRATEGIES TOOLS

Published by:
PROWWESS/UNDP-World Bank Water and Sanitation Program
1818 H Street, N.W.
Washington, D.C. 20433, USA

Produced and distributed by:
PACT, Inc.
777 UN Plaza
New York, NY 10017, USA
Tel.: 1 (212) 697-6222
Fax: 1 (212) 692-9748

A companion videotape, VHS format, NTSC, and PAL, featuring a PROWWESS
Regional Training of Trainers Workshop in Tanzania, is also available from PACT, Inc.

Edited by:
OEF International

Editors
Suzanne Kindervatter, Maggie Range, Nena Terrell
Production Supervisor
Nena Terrell
Editorial Assistants
Leah Hansen, Meg Kimmel, Jacqueline Lucas
Design
Patrice Gallagher, Michele Boris Lytle
Page Composition
Graphix Publishing, Inc.
Photos
PROWWESS/UNDP

Library of Congress Cataloging-In-Publication Data

Srinivasan, Lyra.
        Tools for community participation: a manual for
training trainers in participatory techniques / Lyra
Srinivasan.
#p. #cm. — (PROWWESS / UNDP technical series)
        Includes bibliographical references.
        ISBN 0-912917-20-2
        1. Sanitation, Rural — Citizen participation —
Study and teaching. 2. Rural women — Training of 3.
PROWWESS / UNDP (Program)
1. PROWWESS / UNDP (Program) ll. Title. lll. Series.
TD 157.S67 1990   89 - 77346
363. 72 ' 525 — dc20   CIP

TABLE OF CONTENTS

PART II: 39 PARTICIPATORY TRAINING ACTIVITIES

FOREWORD

The devastation wrought on billions of people through lack of pure water and adequate sanitation is well recognised, and has brought a massive investment of effort and funding (now close to 10 billion U.S. dollars a year) to install pumps, lay water pipes, build latrines and improve sewage systems. Much progress has been made, but major difficulties remain. One such difficulty is low levels of maintenance — many estimates show only 20-40% of services still functioning two to three years after installation. Another is that without major changes in health habits, health impact can be difficult to demonstrate. Finally, funding remains woefully inadequate both for installations and maintenance.

The question therefore is wide open — how can one find replicable ways to ensure the effective and sustainable use of these new services installed at such a high cost? In our search for answers we are inspired also by statements such as the following from "World Development 2000: The Role of UNDP in the 1990's" of February, 1989: "Development has as its ultimate objective the enhancement of human capacities to enable people to manage their own lives and their environment." Our deep belief, strengthened by practice, is that a participatory approach can without question help to match both these technical and human development objectives.

There are many approaches to participatory training. This manual focuses on one such approach, SARAR, which PROWWESS has applied in numerous projects and workshops. Over the years, we have had the deep personal satisfaction of seeing how this approach has inspired enthusiasm in field workers, how it has been adapted and led to new ideas, and how it has helped produce programme results. These results are fully documented in our case studies and other reports, listed at the back of this book. I believe a major strength is the basic simplicity of the approach, which makes it so easy to understand and adapt.

The main purpose of *TOOLS FOR COMMUNITY PARTICIPATION* is to give project staff a sufficiently detailed account of the SARAR approach to help them in

their work. A short video has also been produced as a complement and introduction to the manual.

Participatory training is a field which is rapidly developing. Your comments on this manual are therefore warmly welcome.

Siri Melchior
Manager, PROWWESS/UNDP
1990

ACKNOWLEDGEMENTS

The author wishes to express warm and grateful acknowledgements to the following:

To the former PROWWESS Programme Manager Siri Melchior and her predecessor Sarah L. Timpson, with both of whom it has been a privilege to work and whose vision and commitment to the participatory approach have made possible the rich field experience from which this manual draws.

To the many consultants and colleagues who have collaborated in the 15 training workshops conducted by PROWWESS in Asia, Africa and Latin America and/or in preparing field reports: Noreen Clarke, Colleen Cousins, Andrea Doucet, Mary Elmendorf, Mette Jorstad, Charles Harns, Fran Kealy, Martha Keehn, Jan Northrop, Deepa Narayan-Parker, Jacob Pfohl, Agma Prins, Wendy Quarry, William Sampson, Ron Sawyer, Aminata Traore, Jane Vella, and Jane Wilbur. Their valuable contributions are reflected in the Field Insights interwoven throughout the text and in selected activities in Part II.

To the national core team members, particularly those with whom the author collaborated: Alfred Mondiwa, Dorothy Dhliwayo, Fatima Bopoto, Anunciata Maluto, Jurita Maradzika, and Josephine Mutandiro, (Zimbabwe); Munguti Katui Katua and Rose Mulama, (Kenya); Keiso Matashane and Mamotseli N. Monaheng, (Lesotho); Nafsiah M'Boi and Karen Smith, (Indonesia); Lucie Lubuga and Nancy Masumba, (Tanzania); Indra Gurung and Mina Dayal, (Nepal); Daniel Kadja, Pare Emile, Mariam Ouedraogo, Celestine Some, Rigobert Yago, Elisio Rodrigues, Kadiatou Doumbia, and Pierre Guitton, (Burkina Faso); and to the national trainees and communities associated with the above workshops. They are the ones who provided the proof of the relevance and validity of the participatory approach in their particular setting.

On the SARAR side, to Ron Sawyer, Jacob Pfohl and Chris Srinivasan all three of whom have been closely associated with the author from the inception of SARAR. Their ideas are inseparably interwoven with the methodology.

To all who took time from their busy schedules to review the draft manual and offer suggestions on its editing; their contributions have been most valuable in finalising the text. They include: Timothy Rothermel, Frank Hartvelt, Mina Mauerstein-Bail, Paul Boyd, Michael Sacks, Jennifer Haslett, Lucy Goodhart, Nellie Mathu (UNDP), Joseph Christmas and Gerson Da Cunha (UNICEF), Jan Teun Visscher and Christine van Wijk (IRC), May Yacoob (WASH), Margaret Mwangola (KWAHO), SCF/Zimbabwe, David Walker and Carmen Hunter (World Education), Birgit Madsen of DANIDA (Harare), Rudi Horner (CARE), Khunying Kanok Samsen Vil (GGAT), Ann Bishop (See Hear Productions, Ltd.).

To Nid Kongsamut, Marie McGehee, Rufina Guintu, Martine Villedrouin, Marge Fonyi and Verna Hines who provided valiant assistance at the computer to shape the draft into readable form.

To OEF International and in particular to Suzanne Kindervatter, Maggie Range and Nena Terrell for their painstaking and insightful editing and Patrice Gallagher for doing a creative job in giving the manual its final structure and format.

To all those who kindly provided photographs — namely Ron Sawyer, Deepa Narayan-Parker and Jacob Pfohl. Their contribution has helped bring reality to the issues and experiences reviewed in this book. The photographs come primarily from field activities of PROWWESS.

PART I:

LAUNCHING COMMUNITY PARTICIPATION

A PERSONAL NOTE TO THE READER:

From One Trainer to Another

This book is intended as a discussion starter. It is an invitation to dialogue; an opportunity to stir up ideas among those of us who are trainers. I assume you are a trainer or have a direct or indirect role in making training more relevant and productive. If so, there are a few things you may wish to keep in mind in reading this manual.

This manual focuses on PROWWESS' field experience of adapting and building on the SARAR methodology in the Water Supply and Sanitation Sector (WSS). The application of this "PROWWESS approach" as it has come to be known in the sector, can be seen at closer range in the *Field Insights* interwoven throughout the text. In order to give a unified, in-depth picture, these field insights are limited to only a few of the many contexts in which PROWWESS has been active.

Many of the techniques and activities included in this manual are described in a "how to" step by step fashion. The idea is simply to tell you "this is how we did it". These are descriptions, not prescriptions. They should encourage creativity and innovation by the user: **it is not the technique itself but the underlying principles that matter**.

For this reason I invite your particular attention to the why and how of SARAR activities at the beginning of PART II before going into the detailed procedures for specific activities. Without insight into the design of each activity, the activities could easily become a mere collection of contrived exercises, form without spirit, a "bag of tricks" intended mainly to liven up a training session. That would defeat the purpose.

There is a fundamental issue which we as trainers and/or policymakers and managers face right from the start: How to reconcile an open-ended participatory approach with the need to achieve specific targets in a given sector such as water supply and sanitation. This is a tough question. Can we be honestly open-ended in our approach and at the same time inwardly hope to generate an increased demand for the

particular services our sector offers? What does a water supply technician do, for instance, if the people's priority felt need is for a road or a playground rather than for pumps or latrines? This can be a moral dilemma as well as a practical embarrassment if the agency is expected to set up a certain number of pumps or latrines by year end.

We must anticipate the problem and prepare extension workers to cope with it through dialogue, not manipulation. They need to know what kinds of educational activities can help to broaden the learners' vision beyond "local felt needs", when and how to introduce national sectoral priorities; and how to bring the resources of multi-sectoral teams within reach of local communities so as to respond meaningfully to both agenda.

As you reflect on such issues and explore innovative techniques of your own, we at PROWWESS would be delighted to have you share your experiences with us. Participatory training is such an exciting and growing field and there is so much we can learn from one another.

Lyra Srinivasan

I. COMMUNITY PARTICIPATION IN DEVELOPMENT

Participation: A Strategy For Sustainable Development

Achieving full and effective community participation in development activities is a difficult job and much depends on the way members of the community are approached by field staff, extension workers or technical consultants. The experience of development workers abounds with stories of projects that did not succeed because the intended beneficiaries failed to change behaviour or attitudes that were critical to the projects' success. This type of problem is well known in the Water Supply and Sanitation Sector (WSS). While there are many reasons why costly facilities may fall into disrepair, one critical factor no doubt has been the failure to mobilise the will of the people.

In any sector where the focus is on achieving large scale physical targets within a set time frame, there may be a tendency to treat attitudinal constraints lightly. Project personnel may be aware of community resistance and behaviours which run counter to project objectives, but may believe that these attitudes and behaviours will readily change once the installations or services are in place. They may try several short-cuts to induce behavioural change: pressure from prestigious leaders; pep talks to motivate the community; large community meetings to explain roles and obligations and setting up local committees to enforce those obligations. Often this method does not work. Women especially may be reluctant to take part or to speak up at large meetings, even though they may be the ones who will be expected to carry out most of the relevant tasks.

A Perspective On Women's Roles in the WSS Sector

As the main carriers of water for domestic needs and as the principal moulders of the family's hygienic habits, women's involvement in decision-making in the sector is of critical importance. However, it has taken decades for programme managers to see

15

In order to focus attention explicitly on the special role that women play in relation to water, sanitation and health, the facilitators designed a multi-faceted activity in which a distinct task was assigned to each of three groups. By consolidating the findings of the three groups, participants were able to:

- identify problems that affect rural Zimbabwe communities and rural women in particular;

- examine how women's educational, socio-cultural, economic and health problems influence women's role in water, sanitation and health;

- suggest ways that the community at large or Ministry of Health personnel might help to resolve the most pressing problems affecting women's role in water and sanitation.

The plenary discussion not only contributed to a synthesis on the above items but also provided an opportunity to share the mechanisms or techniques which they had used to arrive at their respective conclusions.

Zimbabwe

the logic and potency of this common sense conclusion. Women have often been regarded primarily as beneficiaries: in exchange for the gift of a pump which would reduce their water hauling workload, they are expected to provide free labour for construction, and to perform routine tasks on a voluntary basis such as attending to the cleanliness of the pump apron and its surroundings.

However, recent field experience of projects assisted by PROWWESS and other donors is demonstrating that rural women, with modest training combined with encouragement and technical support, can make a highly significant contribution to the sector. They have shown themselves capable of fulfilling intelligent and responsible roles in community level planning and management, including needs assessment, site selection, pump maintenance and fund-raising and have exercised intelligence and initiative to increase project effectiveness and to widen support at the local level.

Thus the concept of community participation in the WSS programme is not complete unless rural women, along with their families, play a responsible role in both its planning and management.

When is "Participation" Real Community Participation?

There have been many efforts at community participation. Some work. Some do not. The following cases from the WSS sector illustrate that community participation may be more complex than we think.

The "Cheap Labour" Concept of Participation

In some WSS projects, the community is considered to have participated when it provides free, unskilled labour for construction and donates raw materials "in the spirit of self-help".

The role assigned to villagers is to carry pipes, dig trenches, and perform other unskilled construction tasks. The thinking part (surveying, planning, designing, etc.) is done entirely by engineers and other technically trained personnel. The one benefit derived from this arrangement is obviously the lowering of costs.

Some believe that labour contributions increase the people's identification with the system being built. The assumption is that if they have built a system with their own unpaid labour, they will take pride in it and want to maintain it in good order.

Others contest this assumption. They point out that pride of ownership depends also on what the people's other priorities might be. If the construction project is not a priority for the average community member, labour may be contributed under duress, not voluntarily. If so, then interest in using and sustaining the facility may die after a while.

The "Cost-Sharing" Concept of Participation

In the eyes of other project managers, the key issue is not just cost reduction but cost recovery. They advocate at least token contributions by community members in cash or in kind towards maintenance. People's willingness to invest a part of their meagre resources in maintaining the system (e.g. to pay the local mechanic) is taken as an indication that they value the service and are therefore committed to keeping it in good working order.

Others believe that agreements to maintain a system may not in themselves be a reliable indicator of local commitment. For example, if average community members and, in particular, women have not been involved in decisions concerning the system, they may revert to their old water sources when the pump breaks down rather than contribute towards the cost of repair.

The "Contractual Obligation" Concept of Participation

From another standpoint, neither of the above concepts of community participation is considered adequate to prevent large-scale project neglect, misuse or abuse of installed water supply systems.

Instead of focusing primarily on the cost factor, attempts are made to establish at least a minimal local infrastructure to manage and maintain the system. On the assumption that this infrastructure will be able to generate and sustain local support, project designers have concentrated on three of its elements: local leadership, local committees and locally recruited maintenance volunteers. The assumptions are these:

■ Winning over local leaders will help legitimise the project.

■ Water committees will be able to promote, manage and monitor local contributions and water usage.

■ Through training of volunteer mechanics, pump minders or other local aides, technology can be transferred to the community.

To make these requirements more formal and binding, a contract is often drawn up. The contract spells out in detail what roles and responsibilities apply to each partner in the project (e.g. the government and the community). The community has the option to either accept or reject the terms of the contract or it may even negotiate some changes through the formal power structure of the village.

Sufficient time may be allowed for people to review the terms of the contract among themselves. It is assumed that by assigning management roles to local water committees and by training local mechanics there is greater assurance that the terms of the contract will be fulfilled.

Others, however, question whether this approach sufficiently involves the average villager. They feel that contracts that have been negotiated primarily with village leadership and presented at large village meetings may not be fully understood by the mass community. Therefore, after a while, contributions in labour, cash or in-kind may decline.

Setting up local committees immediately following the first village meeting also runs the risk that the best or the most representative people may not be nominated. Similarly pump caretakers who have been hastily selected may drop out for lack of commitment and accountability to the community at large.

The "Community Decision-Making" Concept of Participation

In the light of the malfunctioning, disuse or abuse of numerous water systems installed in rural communities in recent years, some project managers have come to believe that a substantially different approach than the above is needed to create a strong sense of local responsibility for using the improved resources well, and for sustaining them in good order.

They do not minimise the importance of cost-cutting and cost-recovery measures nor dispute the need for local institutional mechanisms. However, they contend that genuine commitment and widespread support by the community as a whole will only come about if these other measures have been preceded (and continue to be accompanied) by a process of participatory community education and by involving a broad base of the community in decision-making right from the start.

Thus the decision-making requirements apply not only to the male leadership but also—and perhaps particularly—to village women. They point out that women's lack of schooling and literacy skills should not prevent them from making valuable contributions to community decision-making.

There are others who doubt that such an approach can be applied on a large scale. They feel that field staff are not equipped to involve people in this manner and that their training would take too long, be too difficult and cost too much. But, supporters note that participatory training need not be either excessively difficult or costly and contend that, in any case, the long-term benefits would justify the investment.

Questions for Everyone in a Community Participation Project

■ Should one rely on local prestige leaders alone to mobilise local support for project activities? What are the pros and cons?

■ What approach will assure that the community at large voluntarily comes with ideas and solutions, e.g. on how best to constitute work groups or committees, how to pay for services, and so on?

■ Will the experience of working together in physical labour for construction (e.g. digging trenches, carrying loads) suffice to make people identify the programme as their own?

■ If women and other disadvantaged groups do not actively participate in community level discussions, what if anything can or should be done about it and by whom?

■ How soon after a village-wide meeting to introduce the project should a committee be constituted (or identified) to take responsibility for monitoring and supporting local usage and maintenance of the facilities provided?

■ How can technical (hardware) and social (software) inputs best be co-ordinated and integrated so as to encourage and permit full and effective involvement of the people?

■ What are some reliable indicators that community participation in project activities is effective?

■ What educational process should accompany this effort?

■ Which local attitudes, beliefs, or behaviours, stand in the way of full community collaboration in the project?

■ What kind of training do staff need to fulfil this role? Who should be trained and where and when?

Developing a Common Concept of Community Participation

When a heterogenous group of trainees comes together in a workshop, before they receive any orientation or hold any discussions in regard to community participation, it is important to capture each individual's concept of what constitutes valid and feasible involvement of the people. When divergent views are reconciled through dialogue, consensus will take root. This is a principle which applies throughout a participatory workshop.

The principal goal of joint training is to help create a unified vision and a common bond of commitment and competence for enlisting the support of local communities, in particular women.

Often when staff from various sectors and levels come together, they have many preconceived ideas of what community participation means. There are, in fact, many definitions, but it is important that all those close to the project have at least a common understanding of the issues. These are some questions to explore:

- Community Participation: What Do *You* Mean?

- What kind of participation? By whom? Men or women or both?

  In what form? At what levels? In which roles? For what purpose(s)?

- Who will benefit and in what way?

- What needs to be done in order to get that kind of participatory process going?

- What indicators, including people's behaviour, will tell us that the process has been effective?

People may have different answers to these questions. For example, in the WSS sector, the expectations of the engineer may be very different from that of the health educator or the community development officer. The extension agent's perception of which type of community participation is feasible may differ significantly from that of a central office manager who is concerned with costs of installation and maintenance of systems.

Even if everyone cannot agree on common answers, there is great value in people hearing one another's ideas. The ideal is to clarify and refine concepts, reconcile differences and combine ideas into coherent policy.

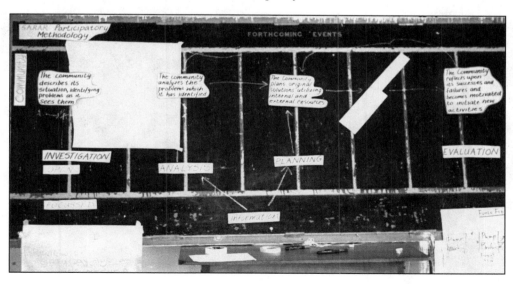

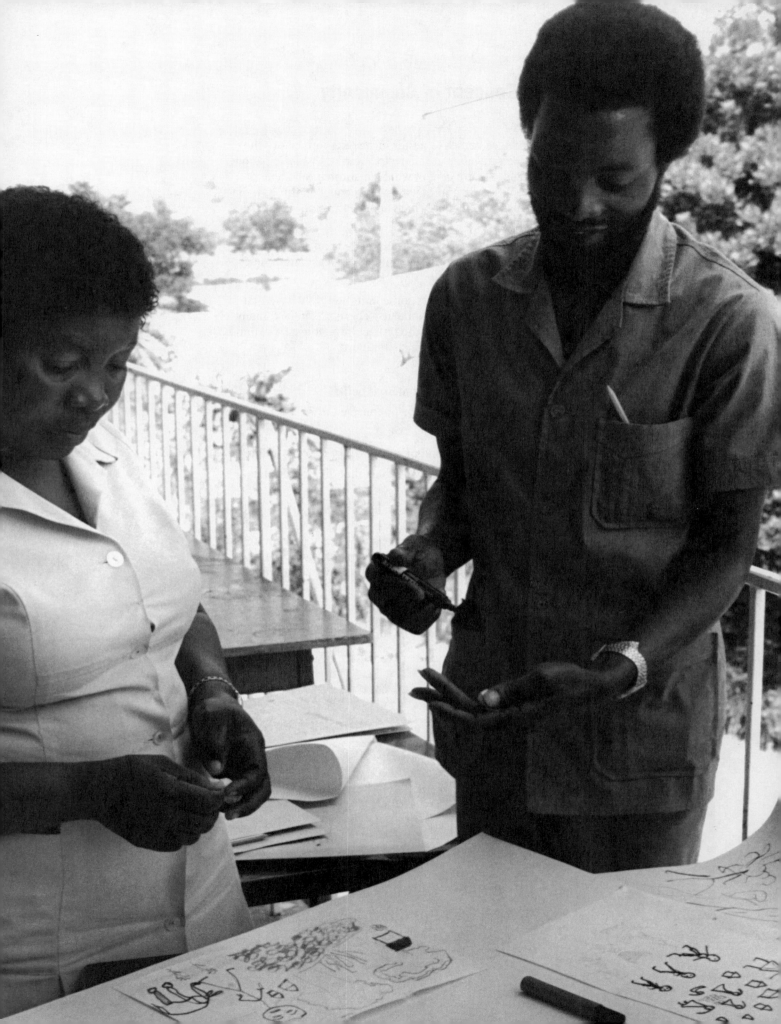

II. PLANNING A PARTICIPATORY TRAINING PROGAMME

How Participatory Training Works

The overriding goal of community participation in the WSS sector is not simply to ensure sustainability of a system by teaching people how to function in a committee or how to fix a pump. Rather, it is to help people develop the outlook, the competence, the self-confidence and the commitment which will ensure a sustained and responsible community effort in the sector and beyond.

If a project comes up against fears, doubts, suspicion, lack of self-assurance or traditional beliefs and values that run counter to the proposed change, a participatory approach can be vital. In communities where such attitudes commonly prevail, behavioural change is unlikely to take place unless a sufficiently sensitive and facilitative approach is used to uncover, examine and address social constraints such as those cited below.

Some Constraints on Participation

- Diffidence in the presence of authority
- Fear of speaking up in group meetings
- Low self-esteem
- Distrust of the motives of those in power
- Reluctance to take risks
- Fear of economic consequences or social loss of face
- Fear of criticism for overstepping customary roles
- Factional differences
- A sense of powerlessness or fatalism
- Lack of experience in working with groups
- Lack of skills in planning and problem-solving

The participatory approach—often known as learner-centred— has evolved over the past decade as a means of helping learners take greater control of their lives and their environment by developing their skills in problem-solving and resource management. Unlike traditional teaching methods which have emphasised the transfer of knowledge, messages or content pre-selected by outside specialists, participatory training such as SARAR focuses more on the development of human capacities to assess, choose, plan, create, organise and take initiatives. These skills can then spill over to many other aspects of the person's life and community.

These aims are synthesised in the following five characteristics of the SARAR approach.

The SARAR Process

Five Characteristics

SELF-ESTEEM

The self-esteem of groups and individuals is acknowledged and enhanced by recognising that they have the creative and analytic capacity to identify and solve their own problems.

ASSOCIATIVE STRENGTHS

The methodology recognises that when people form groups, they become stronger and develop the capacity to act together.

RESOURCEFULNESS

Each individual is a potential resource to the community. The method seeks to develop the resourcefulness and creativity of groups and individuals in seeking solutions to problems.

ACTION PLANNING

Planning for action to solve problems is central to the method. Change can be achieved only if groups plan and carry out appropriate actions.

RESPONSIBILITY

The responsibility for follow-through is taken over by the group. Actions that are planned must be carried out. Only through such responsible participation do results become meaningful.

The adaptation of this approach to the PROWWESS programme has been easy because the underlying aims are compatible. PROWWESS, committed to the involvement of local communities, and particularly women, believes that human capacity development is the key and encourages group responsibility for decision-making and action planning. These are means of ensuring that sectoral improvements correspond to people's priorities and benefit from people's willingness to use them effectively and maintain them in good order.

Who Should Be Involved in Participatory Training?

Considering how greatly the attitudes and skills of field staff can influence local responses, it should not be difficult to recognise a simple truth: the responsibility for the quality of community participation rests, in large measure, in the hands of the trainers. This implies promoting participation not only directly at the community level, but also amongst others who affect the community.

A participatory training programme cannot take place in isolation. Training programmes exist within a project context that involves many other people who affect the project outcomes. All these people must become familiar with the goals of participatory training if the project is to succeed and be sustained.

Trainers are not only those who are on the faculty of training institutions, but also all those who provide in-service guidance and support through field supervision, programme monitoring and evaluation. This includes engineers, technicians, community development officers, agronomists, environmental sanitarians and health assistants.

FIELD INSIGHT

There was some initial concern as to whether or not the workshop objectives were appropriate to the needs of the village women. However, the inclusion of these women in the workshop helped forge a sense of co-operative responsibility between village pump committee members and extension workers and perhaps a rethinking of the contributions that these pump committee members might make as co-trainers at the village level.

The six village women now form a potentially effective training liaison between the extension workers and the other village committee members and non-member villagers. This, with further training and field-level collaboration, may eventually make it easier to hand over project activities to the communities.

This positive outcome is reinforced by a sense of group commitment among trainees from two different Ministries as well as Kenya Water for Health Organisation (KWAHO) extension workers to work in teams for the common goal of successfully involving villagers in their own development.

Kenya

Responsibility also rests with those who make policy decisions affecting training, specifically those who approve or disapprove funds for training resources including representatives of donor agencies who provide the incentives or disincentives which influence the performance of field staff.

Anyone who influences the quality of programme interventions is, in one sense, a trainer and has a stake in community participation.

For participatory training to produce wide impact, policymakers will have to set higher value on qualitative change (e.g. increased community ability to take initiative, shoulder responsibilities, articulate ideas, generate solutions and solve problems).

Clearly, one cannot rely on training alone to change the way extension staff relate to local communities. They need support, guidance and a continuing flow of inspiration from those who make policies and set standards. Without this kind of back-up from policymakers and trainers, they are not likely to innovate or make special efforts to involve people, particularly if "good" performance is judged mainly in quantitative terms (e.g. number of meetings held, demonstrations given, or pump caretakers trained).

The Multi-sectoral/Multi-level Team Building Approach

PROWWESS workshops have often involved many different categories of personnel from other service agencies and sectors. A mixed group serves to broaden limited sectoral perspectives and also encourages a team approach in actual work settings. For example some PROWWESS field-based "training of trainers" workshops have included:

■ Senior and middle level staff from such ministries as Health, Community Development, Women's Affairs, and local government.

■ Social workers from national NGO's.

■ Hardware sector personnel such as engineers, geologists, hydrologists and others from the Ministry of Water Supply.

■ Representatives of donor agencies. (e.g in Zimbabwe, the inclusion of a person

The task was for each of three "functional" groups — i.e., Health Assistants, Health Educators, and Inspectors — to write on rectangles of paper what they considered to be their own professional roles and then what they expect of the cadre immediately above and of the cadre immediately below in the hierarchy. The responses were colour-coded on the board in such a way that each group's perception of its own role was side by side with the other groups' expectations of it. The contrast was often quite dramatic and generated a very lively discussion.

Although the exercise was simple in its design it touched aspects of organisational reality that directly affected everyone involved; and it provoked some of the most animated and spontaneous responses of the workshop.

Zimbabwe

from a donor agency in the participatory workshop, had a significant influence on the entire design of the hardware/software training funded by that donor in 1987.)

It may not be possible to include all these professionals in a formal workshop. But, to build support that will sustain the outcomes of training, the trainer must be prepared to articulate the goals and rationale of a participatory approach to all these groups.

The first time PROWWESS had to train a multi-sectoral group, it had not been anticipated. At practically the last moment, the host country requested that eleven engineers, hydrologists and geologists be allowed to join the workshop as observers. By incorporating them into the group as full participants rather than observers, the trainers themselves learned what a rich experience can result from an interface between technical and socially-oriented personnel. A mixed group does, however, require very special preparation so that the activities hold the interest as well as capitalise on the expertise of all concerned.

Besides multi-sectoral participation, PROWWESS has also had encouraging results with multi-level training, i.e. programmes that involve people who have different levels of authority and responsibility. The simplest type has involved trainers, extension agents and village volunteers, pump minders or other front-line staff who help organise sessions.

A bolder and more complex design of multi-level training has been attempted by bringing together supervisors, trainers, technical specialists and extension workers in a single workshop.

The positive experience of both multi-sectoral or inter-ministerial and multi-level training is illustrated in the preceding *Field Insights* from reports on PROWWESS-assisted workshops in Kenya and Zimbabwe.

Becoming a "Learner-Centred" Trainer

The type of participatory approach described above implies a major change in the relationship between those who traditionally have the prestigious role of teacher or specialist with all the answers, and those who, being largely unschooled, perhaps illiterate, are assigned the passive role of recipients of instruction.

Some technical specialists and project staff in positions of control, may not take too kindly to villagers proposing alternative solutions or expressing reservations concerning their plan of action. As one project director put it, "I don't like being questioned. When I am questioned it lessens my authority."

But in the learner-centred approach, trainers acknowledge and respect the fact that learners, too, have expertise and talents of their own which must be given scope for expression. Only then can they truly function as partners in development.

Participatory training is two-way training, a partnership between the trainer and trainees, by which people discover their own strengths, develop problem-solving skills and together play a more effective role in managing their environment.

As participatory activities help community members learn new skills, the external agent — the trainer —in turn, learns more about the community.

For a trainer, the change from an authoritarian posture to one of partnership is not easy. The participatory process may be considered too time consuming or even seem incompatible with one's job. One engineer put it bluntly: "I am being paid to dig holes. You can do community liaison if you like, but don't interrupt my schedule."

The crux of the problem is well expressed by J. M. Flavier, the Director of the International Institute of Rural Reconstruction (IIRR) in the Philippines, who writes in IIRR's *Rural Reconstruction Review*:

> The first lesson we learned involved the importance of taking enough time. This means having the patience for a lot of dialogue and consultation. Unfortunately, efficiency is often defined as output over time, so the quicker an activity is done, the better it seems. However, many times such efficiency is achieved at the sacrifice of not personally involving the people who are supposedly the target of development efforts.
>
> At first, I was apologetic because of the time it took me in my work to involve villagers. But an Indian philosopher allayed my fears by saying: *"If anyone questions your time-consuming process, give him an egg, and ask him what he wants. For a scrambled egg, ten minutes is plenty of time. For a chick, ah, that takes 21 days!"*
>
> Not only did we learn to consider time but also *timing*. Now, only when the villagers really clamor for more training to have local expertise, do we respond.
>
> The greatest temptation is for a technical staff to set up the whole thing by themselves. But past failures have taught us not to repeat this non-involvement process.

While much can be learned from the hard school of experience, training can provide short-cuts to acquiring skills in participatory techniques and in developing the confidence and the commitment to apply them.

For example, in one country we found that some trainers and extension staff initially considered the participatory approach to be too different from their normal instructional style and they lacked the confidence to apply it. A PROWWESS evaluation consultant reported that they knew a number of techniques but had not used more than one or two for fear that the villagers might consider them too childish or might feel confused or disappointed that no lectures or messages were handed down to them. After a fresh round of field-based training these fears proved to be unfounded. They became comfortable in establishing a dialogue with villagers on an adult-to-adult peer basis.

The truth is that many of us, both trainers and participants, may be products of formal school systems where mastery of content is the goal and the lecture method is

FIELD INSIGHT

One of the groups included two experienced and highly respected extension agents. At the beginning of the Workshop these two often led the discussion and were looked up to by the other participants as models of "the good extension worker". They approached the field visits conservatively, relying on their well-tested expertise. They returned from their first field visit with a long list of community problems based on interviews with selected village people. During the second field visit they experimented with "Unserialised Posters", using them conservatively and, to a large extent, didactically. They came back enthusiastic about the level of participation generated and reported that the community's problems were solved.

The other two groups had taken a greater risk — using the materials more creatively, in a more participatory way and less directively. They had concentrated on more investigative methods. They too came back enthusiastic about the materials and felt they had many options for the next visit.

There was a striking contrast between the methods and experience of the groups (two were made up of people with less extension work experience and the other group included the two experienced extension workers). Though not discussed formally, this contrast generated much reflection on the role of the extension worker.

The two experienced extension workers began to question their old assumptions, seeking out the trainers privately to discuss the experience. By the end of the workshop, the less experienced participants had gained respect for their own abilities and initiatives and the more experienced workers had begun to rethink their tried-and-tested methods. The role of the extension worker as the "facilitator" rather than a "doer" gained increased acceptance among all the participants.

Kenya

the means. The old adage that "teachers tend to teach the way they were taught" holds true in this case. If we have been taught by the lecture method, we may feel more secure using the same method to instruct villagers. That is why PROWWESS Training of Trainers workshops are designed entirely on participatory lines. By the time the group emerges from the experience on the final day, even the most formal members will know, from being deeply involved themselves, what the benefits of the participatory process are in terms of personal growth, greater confidence levels, knowledge gains, and the capability to actually *apply* new skills.

Even so, for most trainers, one workshop is never enough. It may take a series of participatory training experiences before trainers begin to feel truly comfortable in an open-ended, informal, flexible and responsive facilitator-learner relationship.

Because of a serious shortage of trainers with participatory approaches in the WSS sector, developing expertise in participatory training will be greatly valued. Through training other trainers, one can have a significant impact on training programmes and community participation projects in many areas.

Traditional Teaching vs. Participatory Training

In the training field today, the most widely used training approach is what is known as *didactic teaching*. The use of participatory approaches is relatively new.

The traditional Didactic style is a *content-focused* approach in which information is largely passed in one direction from the outside expert to the learner. Social marketing, which involves mass propagation of messages, is a derivative of this approach.

The Participatory style is a *learner-centred* approach in which the focus is on the learners developing abilities and skills to diagnose and solve their own problems. The trainer merely facilitates a process of competency-building and self-discovery for the learners, whose needs, experience and goals are the focus of the training.

Deciding on an approach depends on how trainers diagnose the problem in the first place. Is it merely a question of lack of knowledge (which can be supplied through didactic teaching) or does the solution depend on gaining new insights and achieving fundamental changes in attitudes and behaviours (which can grow out of participatory training)?

Any training programme can include some elements of both approaches, but the hoped-for attitudes and behavioural changes should guide the selection of methodology for each activity.

As participatory training takes hold, PROWWESS has found that the momentum created by a learner-centred approach can pave the way for better utilisation of products or messages being disseminated through more didactic means. The two strategies are complementary and should be planned as such, with emphasis on the participatory learner-centred strategy as the foundation.

Each of the options is discussed below in greater detail. It is up to the trainer to assess their pros and cons and to determine which one is more applicable to a particular situation. However, three points should be kept in mind:

- Each of the styles has some element of participation, but there is a marked difference in the degree and quality of participation each method evokes.

- The fact that they are different does not necessarily mean that one is intrinsically better than the other at all times. They simply serve different purposes.

- The learner's own motivation and readiness may be the single most important criterion to use in determining which strategy is appropriate at any given stage of the learning process.

The choice of a training strategy or approach obviously carries with it budgetary, staffing and administrative implications, all of which need to be supported by a policy commitment. For this reason, it is useful to look closely and in great detail at each option, noting well what purposes it is intended to serve, what its characteristics are, what kind of materials it utilises and what roles it expects staff to play.

The description of options that follows is presented in a straightforward "telling" or didactic fashion. It reflects a personal viewpoint, but one entirely open to questions and challenge. It is not intended to be shared with trainees unless they are equally ready to probe, expand or refute the arguments proposed. At the trainee level, it may be best to begin with participatory activities which engage them in examining these issues on their own, drawing from their own experience. Some examples of such activities will be found in Part II concerning Training Methods and Theory.

Didactic Method

This traditional Didactic style of teaching is sometimes also referred to as the "top-down" or "banking" approach since its primary purpose is the transfer of knowledge.

The didactic style assumes that the learner's main problem is lack of knowledge. Didactic instructors see a gap between what community members know and what they "should" know if they are to make the right connections between cause and effect. The instructor's task then is to fill this knowledge gap.

For example, a health educator may use didactic methods to teach villagers about water-borne diseases or the components of a balanced diet; in the same way, a pump caretaker may be taught the names of different pump parts and the order in which they should be assembled.

The methods and materials used are all geared to transferring technical content from the instructor's mind to the learner's mind. Choice of content is often done on the basis of surveys or studies conducted by researchers. The people may have little or no role in this data collection.

This pre-selected subject matter is then simplified to make it easily understandable by learners. It is divided into segments or units, preferably small enough to be mastered at a single learning session.

Content may also be condensed and presented in the form of simple messages. A number of such messages then make up the curriculum to be covered.

For example, in the WSS sector these messages may include basic sanitation/health guidelines such as the following:

- Use a clean container to draw water.

- Carry the water home in clear jars.

- Store drinking water at home in clean covered vessels.

- Use a clean dipper for taking water out for drinking purposes.
- Keep your yard clean and tidy to prevent flies.
- Use a latrine for defecation.
- Dispose of children's feces in a safe way.
- Wash your hands often with water and soap.

Adapted from Working Together for Better Water, *Foundation for International Training, Toronto, Canada, 1984.*

These messages may be organised into a logical sequence. To ensure that they will be presented in exactly the same order, they may be numbered, printed and bound together in the form of a flip chart.

To reinforce the mastery of content, instructors may employ techniques such as the following:

- use different media to make the messages more memorable;

- consistently praise "right" answers and discourage "wrong" answers;

- apply external incentives or disincentives or exclusion from benefits. These can include such incentives as certificates, prizes, attention by VIPs, example of role models; such disincentives as fines or warnings of negative consequences if behaviour is not brought in line with the given message, e.g. "If you do not build a latrine, you may all suffer from diarrhoea" or exclusion from benefits such as "Only those prepared to pay can use the pump."

The advantage of the directive approach is that it simplifies the instructor's task of teaching subject matter. For example, it is easy for a field worker to teach from a flip chart on latrine construction or child weaning foods because the instructions on what to say are printed at the back of each picture. The instructor asks questions or gives assignments that will test whether the message has been received and remembered. Thus many hundreds of field workers can be sent out to villages after short training, armed with flip charts, posters and other materials. It is also easy to mass produce such materials since they are standardised.

A serious disadvantage is that the simple transfer of information from the instructor to the learners seldom assures the latter will change their behaviour. Often the villagers can recall the messages perfectly but fail to adopt them in practice. If the instructor is seen as an authority figure the people's response may be polite and deferential but often non-committal.

Unless villagers are very highly motivated to acquire the specific knowledge and skills offered, they may not easily buy into the programme when approached in a top-down manner.

Social Marketing

This is a variant of the didactic style of more recent origin, greatly influenced by modern advertising and sales techniques. Here, also, the emphasis is on the transfer of information believed to be needed by the people.

For example, health is considered to be a "marketable commodity" and, accordingly, a number of health messages are selected and tested to see if they are understandable by the people and compatible with the prevailing culture and perspectives of community members.

The original messages or recommendations are chosen on the basis of their technical soundness; by testing them intensively among small groups of people (called "focus groups"), preferably of the same cultural and socio-economic background as the target group, the messages are refined and modified to make them more palatable. To that extent, villagers may be said to participate in the shaping of messages. For example, they may suggest a different picture or a change in colours or a different way of working the message to make it fit better into their local context or they may comment on the substance of the recommendation itself. What results from this process is a synthesis of new and traditional ways of doing things, thus making the message more persuasive.

On that basis, a larger campaign is then "launched" to "sell" the new idea or practice to the people using persuasive marketing techniques; the expectation is that the new message will be accepted and will result in behavioural change.

Thus social marketing is clearly much more flexible in its approach than conventional didactic teaching. The underlying structure, however, is similar: both strategies are built around pre-selected content and both disseminate recommendations or "prescriptions for action."

While the traditional didactic style is now generally recognised as having serious limitations if used as an exclusive or main strategy at the village level, social marketing has aroused considerably more interest in recent years. It has attracted the attention of some multinational donors because it seems to hold promise of massive impact in a relatively short time. Although this benefit has yet to be substantiated across the board, social marketing has some obvious advantages over conventional didactic teaching.

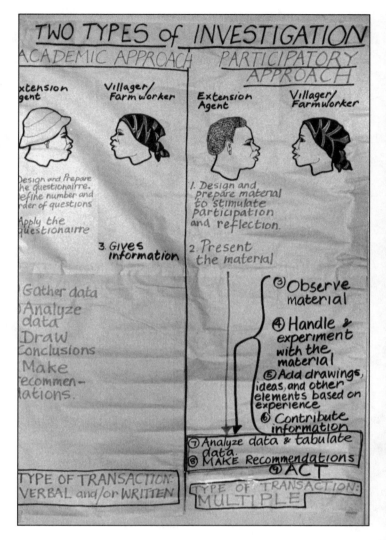

Participatory Training

The learner-centred, participatory approach is the more open and flexible of the two main options being reviewed here. Since an analysis of this approach (through PROWWESS' experience with SARAR) is the main thrust of this manual, we need not go into great detail at this point but simply highlight the major ways it differs from didactic teaching and social marketing.

Participatory training fosters a process of human development, but it does not take place in a vacuum. It is supported through a number of practical experiential activities which engage learners in creative problem-solving and provide opportunities for new forms of self-expression. By being involved in a variety of new ways, learners discover talents and abilities which they never knew they had. Their self-confidence increases enormously. The quality of their participation accordingly improves through the *cumulative effect* of several activities. Sometimes it improves by leaps and bounds depending on the enthusiasm generated in the peer group and the support forthcoming from the external intervention agency.

While an agency's field staff may be bound by specific sectoral interests — as in water supply, sanitation, nutrition or agriculture, — the content of learning is not prescribed by specialists as a set body of knowledge to be imparted to villagers or as a package of messages which they are to be persuaded to adopt. On the contrary, the field staff begin with activities which enable them to learn from and about the villagers.

Learning sessions are therefore structured in the form of problem-solving activities or tasks requiring teamwork and open peer discussion. While the field worker or trainer provides the simple structure of the problem-solving activity or task, the content comes mainly from the learners, drawn from their own rich experience of life. This increases the relevance of the learning and gives them self-assurance in practising problem-solving skills.

III. ORGANISING THE WORKSHOP: RESOURCES AND LOGISTICS

Why a Workshop?

Training of trainers is a starting point for creating a new outlook on training in a participatory manner. When trainers are exposed to participatory training — in fact, when they are thoroughly immersed in it through a full-scale experiential workshop — they are likely to want the same for the personnel under their charge.

Minimal and Optimal Requirements

Duration of the Workshop

The workshop can be scheduled for nine to twelve days, although ten is ideal with one day's break. This allows some participants to return home over the weekend or the time can be used to prepare for the field work.

The description below presents an ideal set up for a 9 — 12 day workshop which may not always be feasible particularly for voluntary organisations with limited resources. Keeping this in mind, a trainer can make the adjustments appropriate to a given situation, as long as the quality of the training process is safeguarded. If field work cannot be arranged, the workshop could be condensed into 5 days or at a push even reduced to 3 days.

The following pointers from PROWWESS experiences are stated as guidelines; they are not absolute prerequisites but useful to reflect on.

Selecting Participants

The number of participants should preferably not exceed 27; the ideal is around 24 so that three small groups can be formed. This allows for closer interaction among participants. To the extent possible, the group should include different categories and/or levels of workers involved in the sector.

Regarding the appropriate mix of participants, please refer to the section "Who Should Be Involved In Participatory Training?", p. 22 , for information about how PROWWESS has conducted multi-level and multi-sectoral training.

It is important that all participants should commit themselves to attending full-time, starting from Day One and remaining until the end of the final session. It disrupts the process if some participants arrive late and/or leave early.

Selecting Resource Persons

Participatory Trainers

A workshop can be conducted by one facilitator but it is preferable to have two, both well versed in participatory approaches. They will need to take turns at fulfilling the complementary roles of conducting sessions and monitoring the process and its impact.

A small core team of 2 to 5 experienced host national trainers will be needed to work closely with the facilitators in planning and conducting the workshop, if the facilitators are expatriates. They are needed in particular to ensure that each activity is relevant, useful, and culturally appropriate in the local context. They should also take responsibility for such items of the programme which they can comfortably handle under the guidance of the main facilitator.

Local Artist(s)

For the activities listed in the manual, some will require the use of one or two local artists both before and during parts of the workshop. Since the use of visual material as stimuli for discussion is one effective way to involve villagers, the artist's role is vital for developing the initial momentum. However, if you have an adequate supply of open-ended visuals on hand (i.e. pictures that are open to interpretation and can be feasibly used) and if your budget is limited you may want to do without the full-time artist.

In any event, both workshop participants and villagers should be encouraged to produce their own drawings which an artist can later reproduce for wider use. Sample drawings for local adaptation are provided with the corresponding activity in Part II.

Secretarial Support

The support of at least one secretarial assistant is desirable during the programme. This helps the trainers to be free to concentrate on the training itself rather than on logistics. With the help of a secretary, much of the material generated during the workshop (including group reports) can be typed and distributed to participants before the workshop ends.

Selecting a Location

Participatory programmes for training of trainers and of project staff should prefera-bly be field-based. In that way, trainees can have first-hand opportunities to determine how the participatory process works at the village level. They do so by working with real people in real villages on problems which have immediacy to the community. Thus a clear relationship is established between concrete village situations and the participatory approach to problem-solving.

It is therefore strongly recommended that the main workshop be held in a rural or semi-rural area where the participants will confront village reality. The locale should be residential and far removed from the participants' work situations. Simple accommodations in the vicinity of potential field sites is better than more lavish arrangements at an urban hotel. Pre-planning, however, could take place in the capital city.

Planning Field Work

For field work purposes, participants should have easy access to three small villages, which have comparable socio-economic conditions and are roughly equidistant from the workshop site (or one large village in which three groups could work without overlap).

In addition, the villages selected should either:

■ be in an area which already has or is scheduled to have a technical assistance programme related to the main theme of the workshop (in this case WSS), or

■ have access to an agency, such as an NGO, which, having participated in the field work, is prepared to move in quickly to do follow-up.

First contact the leadership of all three areas for permission to visit the communities and conduct brief participatory education sessions with village members.

Arranging Transport

If the three field sites are not within walking distance, arrangements for transport needs to be made for all three groups, each accompanied by one or more members of the core team, as observers. Since the use of hired vehicles and drivers can be expensive, this expenditure for transport must be carefully planned, budgeted and monitored.

Equipment and Supplies

The following items are useful to have on hand although PROWWESS workshops have on occasion managed with less:

- A typewriter,
- typing paper,
- large sheets of "newsprint" or other poster-size blank paper,
- felt pens,
- thumb tacks,
- masking tape or other adhesive,
- art materials (poster colours, brushes, etc.),
- scissors,
- staplers,
- glue,
- notebooks,
- pencils and erasers.

Desirable items include equipment for duplicating materials developed during the workshop, e.g. a mimeograph machine if a photocopier is not available, and an eyelet puncher to produce flexi-flans.

IV. DESIGNING THE PARTICIPATORY WORKSHOP

Trainer Guidelines

In the design of participatory workshops, three characteristics are critical to their success:

1. Sessions Reflect or Simulate Community Level Process

In the PROWWESS training of trainers programmes, sessions are designed so as to simulate a community level process as closely as possible. In other words, a nine-day workshop attempts to put trainers through a sequence of structured participatory experiences similar to those which might evolve over nine weeks or even nine months at the community level. The participants will therefore understand "process" by experiencing it themselves.

2. Trainees Analyse Training Activities and Tools in Terms of the Behavioural/ Attitudinal Responses They Evoke

Participants also learn to analyse the different workshop activities and tools in terms of the type and quality of responses evoked, e.g. the extent of active involvement in decision-making. In this way, they gain insights into how the educational approach they choose can influence participation. They learn how they can stimulate and support the process of human development.

3. Trainees Test Participatory Methods in Real-Life Village Situations

When participants do their field work in actual villages as part of their workshop experience, they get living proof that the approach works in real life contexts. They gain insight into process through direct feedback from the villagers.

The above pointers could be restated simply as three guidelines which PROWWESS has found to be essential for success.

1. Make training highly experiential; that way participants will learn about process by living it.

2. Have participants learn to analyse educational activities and tools in terms of the impact on learners' attitudinal or behavioural growth. They will then know how to design and use techniques to stimulate the desired growth process.

3. Include field testing of participatory techniques in actual villages. That way participants will see for themselves that the process is easy to initiate and produces positive changes in learner attitudes and perspectives in real life.

Pre-planning at the Country Level

The importance of holding a pre-planning session locally cannot be overemphasised. It is the trainer's key to making the main workshop relevant and to leaving behind a core team of national trainers who can replicate the process on their own at a future date. The purpose of the pre-planning session is to develop the overall design and programme of the workshop. This is done jointly by the facilitators and the core team. In so doing, it serves to bring about a unified vision, as mentioned earlier, and a sense of common purpose and commitment to teamwork.

This mini-workshop, usually three to five days, can be scheduled approximately a week before the main training programme. This allows a break of a few days after the pre-planning session to organise materials, have art work completed, and make final arrangements, including preparations for the field work.

The pre-planning workshop is actually a preview of the types of activities that will be conducted in the main training programme.

The core trainers are first exposed to a number of experiential training activities themselves so that, having had direct exposure to the SARAR process, they can help to make decisions as to what should or should not be included in the programme. Ideas for alternative activities or materials are also generated and rehearsed.

As a planning tool, proposed activities are written on small pieces of paper and attached tentatively to a newsprint "calendar". Decisions as to whether and when to use them can then be made or revised without having to re-do an entire schedule. Core team members are reminded that whatever sequence of activities is planned at this point has to be extremely flexible, to allow for any changes needed as the team interacts with participants at the main workshop, in accommodation to their interests and pace of work.

If circumstances permit, a final "dress rehearsal" can be scheduled two or three days prior to the workshop. This provides an opportunity to review final plans, clarify roles and build team spirit and confidence.

It is not always easy to explain to local organisers why PROWWESS does not believe in sending out a standard pre-packaged workshop programme. However, to do so would deprive the national core team of an invaluable opportunity to get involved directly in designing the workshop; thus, there would be a real risk of the programme becoming an imposition, irrelevant to the realities of the country. Furthermore, PROWWESS believes that those who will later attend the main workshop as trainees should have a say in which issues they want addressed during their training.

Setting Objectives

The following is a compilation of objectives from several different workshops conducted by PROWWESS. Trainers can choose among them or create their own. Depending on the evaluation framework for the programme, it is useful to set clear behavioural or competency-based objectives, such as "Participants will be able to identify three characteristics of participatory training." Here however they are stated in terms of what the trainer sets out to do.

Objectives should be reviewed and modified at each workshop in consultation with the participants. This is done on the very first day, but only after the participants have expressed and discussed their own expectations about the outcomes of the workshop. In this way, the training programme becomes the property of both the participants and the trainer in contrast to traditional trainer-directed programmes.

To involve participants in defining and/or refining workshop objectives see the Activity "Expressing Hopes and Fears" (*Human Development* Activities in PART II).

Sample Trainer Objectives

- To create awareness at different service levels of the importance of using participatory principles and strategies in implementing community-based WSS programmes.

- To jointly train personnel from different Ministries and development agencies so as to promote team relationships and help unify their vision and approach to community level work.

- To help participants learn to differentiate among a wide range of participatory strategies, techniques and tools so as to know when, how, why and with whom to use them.

- To help them develop a deeper understanding of the learner-centred participatory approach in terms of personal growth, group cohesiveness, and capacity for practical problem-solving.

- To review ways of overcoming major impediments to the full involvement of local community members, in particular, women, in the planning and implementation of WSS programmes and facilities.

- To provide participants with guided opportunities to design their own alternative educational materials related to WSS.

- To assist them in analysing their real life work situations so as to identify aspects which could benefit from the use of participatory techniques.

- To assist trainers to develop skills as facilitators in planning and conducting similar training on their own.

- To engage them in planning possible follow-up activities at the country level using insights and skills gained at the workshop.

Components in the Workshop Design

Opening and Closing Day Formalities

In many countries it is customary to start and close training activities with a formal ceremony presided over by a high official or other dignitary. But a formal opening can make it more difficult to switch to the informal relaxed climate needed for participatory training. With a little explanation, however, most national agencies are ready to forego the opening ceremony in the interest of maximising the benefits of the workshop. However, a closing ceremony should definitely be scheduled. By that time, participants will be confident and excited about participatory methods and can use the occasion to share their experience and plans with invited guests.

While the workshop design is always tentative, the programme falls generally into three phases:

1. The Immersion Phase (5 to 7 days)

The first three or four days may be devoted to total immersion in participatory methodology. Each activity after being experienced is thoroughly analysed and evaluated. (See the section on "Simple Daily Evaluation Techniques and Activities" p.45)

■ Organising Small Groups and Choosing Villages

On the first day, participants organise themselves into three smaller groups through a self-selection process. See "Forming Subgroups" below. Each of these groups picks one of the three villages for its field work.

■ Visiting the Villages

During this Immersion Phase, the village visits may begin. The initial field trip to the villages may take place as early as the first day, perhaps in the afternoon. The number and timing of such field visits is left as flexible as possible to give participants autonomy in decision-making.

■ Designing Tools to Use in the Villages

By the end of the Immersion Phase, participants should be ready to apply the same principles in designing activities and materials of their own. Two to three days may be needed for participants to design and test some tools they plan to use at the village level in the second phase. The planning and preparation of these activities is left entirely in the hands of each group. It is their opportunity to apply what they have learned and make autonomous decisions.

To ensure that these tools are grounded in reality, their themes are drawn directly from the village field visit conducted during the first few days of the programme.

PROCEDURES

■ Forming Subgroups

Three subgroups should be formed early in the workshop and maintained for all key activities, especially the Field Trip. (For many other activities, the composition and size of the subgroups is deliberately changed so that participants can mix freely and get to know one another in a variety of combinations.)

The three subgroups should be self-selected. Give participants special name tags that have been colour-coded to indicate their professional specialty and/or category or place of work. Ask them to fix name tags on the blackboard under any one of the three letters, A, B, and C.

No subgroup should have more than one-third the total number of participants and no subgroup should have a predominance of any one category or specialisation or geographic area. The colour-coded name tags help to visually determine any imbalance within the groups.

If the groups are unbalanced, ask for volunteers to move from one group to another. While this self-selection process does take longer than group assignments by management, the end result of self-selection is that the subgroups develop and maintain a strong sense of identity and feel individually responsible for the quality of their team effort.

In the same way, the villages in which they will do their field work are selected by lottery.

As the subgroups plan for the village visits, trainers should generally observe a strictly hands-off policy, leaving the groups alone to make their own decisions and discover resources within their own membership.

FIELD INSIGHT

One activity, done in two subgroups, was the building of three-dimensional village maps.

To make their maps, or models, participants used all kinds of odds and ends such as (clay, sand, cardboard, buttons, shells, cotton, fabric and other materials) contributed by local trainers, supplemented by other materials collected by the participants themselves.

Each village team was asked to draw a map depicting the ward and to compile a list of characteristics, resources and problems. The volunteers were critical to this process as they alone knew the village. They were to instruct agency representatives about their site. Each group then reported its findings to the others. The activity went well with virtually every village volunteer taking active part.

The point in introducing the map activity was to engage the group in an intensive, highly creative self-directed experience. It would serve at least two purposes:

■ to establish, in their own minds, through their own living experience, the high level of energy, enjoyment and creativity that can be generated by a participatory approach in which the facilitators' role is minimal and

■ to enable the subgroup members themselves to share their village experience in the process of creating their maps and to use the end product as a concrete take-off point for subsequent activities.

Each group presented its village map. Water problems represented included:

■ dry river

■ dirty waterhole

■ an untapped spring

■ borehole with a broken handpump, village waiting for government to repair it

Out of these presentations came the idea to use this activity in the villages, to let the villagers build their own maps to tell about their village, and to share their perceptions of problems and distances associated with water.

Indonesia

■ Getting to Know the Village Reality

Participants should visit their village as soon as feasible after the beginning of the workshop, usually during the first two days. They are free to plan follow-up visits for other days on their own as needed. During these visits, they can identify issues, concerns or specific problems which are of special significance to the local people and are recognised by them as priority problems. This is a type of informal baseline assessment.

■ Gearing up for a Learning Encounter

From the baseline information obtained (preferably in a participatory way), each subgroup then selects a topic or topics and plans one or more learning experiences around those themes. The groups are expected to conduct these learning experiences by arrangement with villagers on an appointed day and at a time and place convenient to community members, particularly the women.

It should be made clear to the villagers by both the trainers and the participants that the teams will be in the village in a learning capacity and have nothing to offer the community except some enjoyable moments together through which learning can mutually take place. If stated candidly, this position is generally acceptable to village community members.

Almost invariably after the experience, they have expressed their pleasure at the opportunity to participate in this novel way. The feelings of the group at the end of an African village session were best expressed in the comments of a village chief: "We were like an axe that needed to be sharpened." Village women in Nepal said: "Now we understand that we can solve our own problems and make our own materials. We gathered here from different places and we worked together. It forces us to think and gain knowledge."

In preparing for the follow-up visit, each subgroup may use simple questions such as the following:

■ Guide for Planning a Participatory Session

What will be the central subjects or theme(s) of the session?
Who will participants be? How many?
What will be the venue? When? Where?
What will be the objectives of the session?
Which techniques or materials will you use?

Each group then prepares a statement of the step-by-step procedures it will follow in conducting the session. Special attention is given to keeping the facilitator's role minimal and ensuring maximum learner participation. Materials actually needed for use at the session are then prepared.

2. THE ENCOUNTER PHASE (2 TO 3 DAYS)

■ Dress Rehearsal for Village Visits

This phase begins with "dress rehearsals". Subgroup teams critique the activities they propose to conduct in their selected village and the materials they have prepared to stimulate community participation. Resource persons may share in the critique.

■ Field Testing in the Villages

Each group field tests its educational approach with an actual village group and evaluates the response. By the next day all three groups must have analysed their field experience and reported back to the plenary.

PROCEDURES

Teams are given at least a day to plan, rehearse and get a critique of their prepared session. On the day agreed upon by the villagers, each subgroup conducts its session. The process is monitored by a few of the participants who have been especially briefed to observe the degree and quality of people's participation. This field experience usually results in a feeling of elation among participants upon seeing the response of the villagers. If the groups initially had fears about using a new methodology, this fear is minimised by seeing that all the groups enjoyed some measure of success. There is great willingness to learn from each other.

3. EVALUATION AND FOLLOW-UP PLANNING PHASE (2 DAYS)

The last phase is for evaluation and planning of follow-up activities. It prepares the participants for their re-entry into their normal programme or policy functions and for adaptation of what they have learned to their national context.

This Phase ends with a formal closing ceremony. At this time, participants can share their experience with a much wider audience including their agency's senior personnel, donor agency representatives and local authorities.

FIELD INSIGHT

We were the first to arrive at the meeting place. About 30 women gathered within the half hour. The village volunteer and an agency trainer welcomed the women and briefly described the purpose of the visits. The volunteer then put in the middle of the circle of women the picture of the baby with diarrhoea, a problem the villagers had selected as a priority on our previous visit. She then passed out pictures of the causes of diarrhoea and asked the women if they could identify any factors in the pictures that caused the disease.

Slowly women began to exchange pictures and to discuss links between the pictures and the disease. One or two older women in the group were knowledgeable and gave the other women good information. The following exchange was typical: One woman looked at a picture of a woman washing in a stream where animals were immersing themselves in the water. She said, "This water is dirty and using it causes sickness". Another woman took the picture from her hand and said, "Why is this water dirty? It looks clean to me". The first woman then explained that the animals were dirty, defecated in the water, had diseases and parasites, etc. The second woman nodded and said, "Oh, I see, that *is* dirty water".

Next, the volunteer gave the group the set of pictures of prevention strategies. She asked them if they could match causes and prevention. Again women began to decode the pictures and try different matches. During the lively discussion, the trainers kept quiet. When matching had been completed the women selected one of their group members to explain their choices. She moved back and forth describing causes and preventative measures, sometimes receiving help from her companions. Everyone enjoyed the exercise and participated actively.

Nepal

FIELD INSIGHT

A lot of people were gathered at Felton Farm compound. The group of participants which visited the farm prepared to demonstrate to the community how to create stories using *flexis* on a flannel board. After demonstration, a number of people volunteered to create their stories using the method. Three people presented their stories. The stories aroused discussion and debate among the community members present and led them to talk about problems they face on the farm, like housing, sanitation and health services. By the end of the session the facilitators were pleased that the objectives of the activities were achieved while the community was happy because their problems and felt needs had been discussed and some solutions proposed through the activity.

Zimbabwe

The Training Team was pleased to discover the degree to which participants were prepared to rely on their own resources and resourcefulness to produce training materials. The use of cut-outs from Kenya posters and the enormous success of the Healthy/Unhealthy Baby cut-out material in the communities probably helped considerably. Another related outcome demonstrated during the follow-up session was the degree to which the participants came to view each other as resources and their desire to form inter-institutional multi-disciplinary teams for follow-up work in the field. For example, the extensionists and village women said they needed to learn more about diseases and other health/sanitation-related issues. The public health technicians, who already know a good deal about these matters, now have a much better idea how they can transmit technical information using a less directive approach. This realisation naturally led to a sharing of ideas on how field teams might be composed.

Kenya

PROCEDURES

Each group is expected to report on its experience at the very next plenary session using a three-question guide:

- What did you plan?
- What happened?
- What did you learn?

The third question includes what one might do differently the next time around, based on this experience.

Not all the group reports need to be in narrative form. Some may use role plays to demonstrate what happened. Others may illustrate their reports with flexi-flans or symbolic objects. All media are acceptable. Creativity must have free play.

To consolidate this experience, the group may be given a set of guidelines such as the following which, when read vertically, spell **SUCCEED.**

SOME GUIDELINES FOR PLANNING PARTICIPATORY ACTIVITIES

If you want to SUCCEED, you need to:		If you do, you will:
S	Set a brief, clear task rather than lecture or ask questions.	Share power.
U	Use hands-on, multi-sensory materials rather than rely only on verbal communications.	Broaden the base of participation.
C	Create an informal, relaxed climate.	Equalise status.
C	Choose a growth-producing activity.	Draw out talents, leadership, mutual respect.
E	Evoke feelings, beliefs, needs, doubts, perceptions, aspirations.	Ensure relevance.
E	Encourage creativity, analysis, planning.	Enhance personal confidence, self-esteem, skills, resourcefulness.
D	Decentralise decision-making.	Develop capacity for practical action.

FIELD INSIGHT

One technique used to consolidate what was learned from the field work experience is called *Success Analysis*, developed by consultant Agma Prins. This structures group reports so that deeper understanding of the process takes place and commitment is created. Following the pre-liminary reports in whatever form, participants are asked to think about the following questions:

Which aspects of the field visit were most successful?

What factors most contributed to this outcome?

What were the major difficulties encountered? How might these have been avoided?

What recommendations would you make for the future?

This approach has several advantages. It focuses on the positive aspects of the experience before passing critical judgement over what might have been avoided or done better. More im-portantly, it calls attention to the fact that using people's participation as the main criterion, there are success elements in every one of the experiences although the means used may be different. The feeling that one is on the right track helps to strengthen the resolve to keep going.

Kenya

V. SIMPLE DAILY EVALUATION TECHNIQUES AND ACTIVITIES

In the SARAR approach, evaluation activities accompany every step of the training process, using a wide variety of methods. While participants are evaluating their own performance, they are simultaneously evaluating the tools utilised in training.

Daily evaluation serves several purposes. It provides guidance to trainers and participants alike on the relevance of the activities, the level of interest aroused, the evocative power of the tools and the issues surfacing from group discussion. It also demonstrates the extent to which participatory principles are understood in each exercise and the degree to which any behavioural changes indicate personal growth, organisational capacity and leadership skills.

Frequent evaluation exercises enable group members to observe and measure their own progress. In addition, by beginning each day with the brief review and group assessment of the previous day's activities, participants gain a sense of the continuity of the learning process. They also come to realise the importance of continuous reflection and of timely feedback in a training programme that aims to be genuinely responsive to the adult learners' own interests and needs.

The evaluation exercises we have used include ballot boxes and the "Pocket Chart" Activity (*Methods/Investigative*), grids and checklists, brainstorming (factors that help or inhibit participation), feedback (via drawings, flexi-flans or role plays), opinion polling, video tape playback, and using everyday objects and scenes in a symbolic way (e.g. using a river to symbolise the course of the workshop from start to finish). If workshop participants are to learn to design their own participatory training activities, one method is to take apart several activities and see how they are structured and what purpose they serve.

What follows here are some of the forms of evaluation used in PROWWESS workshops.

The Action Words Behaviours List

This analysis focuses on the learner behaviours evoked by an activity. The facilitator asks participants to name several of the activities completed and to select two or three which are very different in design. The participants, in subgroups, analyse how they behaved during the course of the activity and note their behaviours by making a list of action words.

For example, during the opening ceremony, what action words might describe their roles? The list begins with "We...." followed by the action word, such as "...listened", "...observed", "...clapped" and so on.

The verb list for another activity might be very different. For example, action words for a mapping activity might include: we planned, we discovered, we compared, we selected, we discussed, we decided, we compromised, we worked hard, and so on.

When several activities are analysed in this way, participants become aware that the desired behaviours can be stimulated or evoked by many different techniques and materials, but not by all. This shifts attention from the technique itself to the principles on which it is based and the process it generates.

The Overall Design Review Grid

In a workshop that is heavily activity-based, participants may need help to see how all of these activities fit into an overall design which has larger objectives than the individual exercise. Without this sense of direction, scope and organisation, participants may get confused by moving from activity to activity without knowing how they fit together.

For this reason, they are shown a large review grid in which the activities of the

Activities	Community Participation					Human Development				Methods						Practical Application			
	Quality of	Benefit of	Constraints to	Strategies for	Roles in	Personal Identity	Human Relations	Group Strength	Team Work	Creative	Investigative	Analytic	Planning	Informative	Evaluative	Experience-sharing	Follow-up Planning	Unified Vision	Intersectoral Coordination
1																			
2																			
3																			
4																			
5																			
6																			
7																			
8																			
9																			
10																			

day (or the week) are listed in the horizontal columns and the generic purposes are listed in the vertical columns. These purposes are grouped under headings, such as Community Participation, Human Development, Methods and Practical Application.

The Review Grid is posted in a prominent place on the first day of the training programme. Each new activity is added to the Activities Column so that participants can keep track of the programme as it develops. Then selected activities are analysed in terms of how well each helps to achieve the purposes listed in the vertical columns of the grid. By analysing several items in this way, the group begins to realise that it is the combined effect of all the activities that counts. It is only necessary for the trainer to conduct this type of review in plenary session for the first few activities. Once the process is understood, participants can apply the grid on their own.

The Learner-Centred Design (LCD) Criteria

The purpose of the LCD Criteria is to determine if a learning activity at the community level can fully involve adult learners. Criteria are listed below as a set of questions on the left and as a set of cues on the right. You may use either one.

Learner-Centred Design Criteria Questions	LCD Clues: Did the activity include elements of:	1	2	3	4	5
Was it enjoyable?	Enjoyment					
Did it involve sharing of experiences?	Experience-sharing					
Was it a hands-on activity?	Hands-on activity					
Was it a multi-sensory experience?	Multi-sensory experience					
Did it require use of creativity and imagination?	Creative imagination					
Did it involve analysis?	Analysis					
Did it involve problem-solving?	Problem-solving					
Did participants have to make their own decisions?	Decision-making					
Did it require assessment of alternative solutions?	Solution-finding					
Were participants engaged in planning?	Planning					
Did participants assume different roles and responsibilities?	Assumption of roles and responsibilities					
Did the group do any evaluation?	Evaluation					
Did the activity require clarification of concepts?	Learning from experience Conceptualizing					

Self-Evaluations:

Using the Symbolism of the Environment

The Mountain Evaluation Sheet, developed by Charles Harns and Jan Northrop, was used in Nepal for participants to evaluate their own progress during the workshop. This self-evaluation technique provides feedback to the participants and staff on how individuals rate their own achievements and progress along the river banks winding between mountain ranges which symbolise constraints.

The form is distributed at the end of the day. In the interest of safeguarding anonymity participants are asked to put a mark or symbol on the form which only they would be able to identify as their own. The trainer averages the marks and later shares them with the group.

In such exercises, it is particularly important that participants not limit themselves to mastery of knowledge or to the number of techniques in which they have become skilled. For example, in the PROWWESS workshop in Nepal, participants became aware that underlying these practical achievements, there had been a subtle but very real inner change. They emerged feeling good about themselves, about each other as members of a team, about the task ahead and about their personal capacity to decide, plan and act on their own behalf.

Nepal Workshop Participants Self-Evaluation Chart

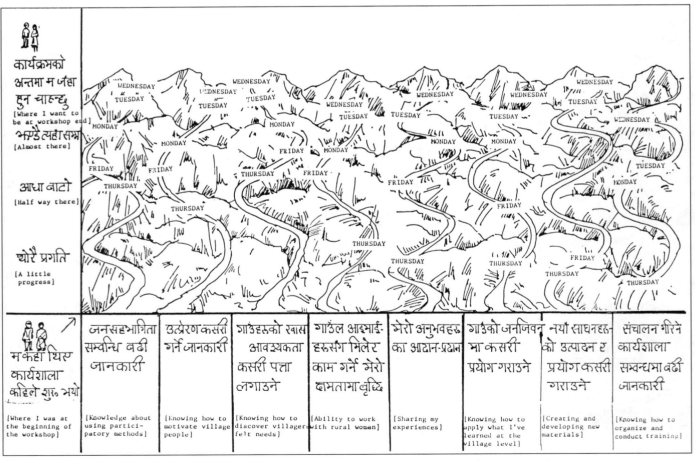

Two other evaluation forms focus more on the participants' day-to-day involvement in the training process and on their feelings about the quality of participation, of learning and of growth as a person. These forms are attached herewith, not as models, but as examples of a range of tools which can be utilised for this purpose.

My Participation Diary

ACTIVITY _____	Day 1			Day 2			Day 3			Day 4			Day 5			Day 6			Day 7		
	No	Some	Yes	No	Some	Yes	No	Some	Yes	No	Some	Yes	No	Some	Yes	No	Some	Yes	No	Some	Yes
I listened actively to what others said.	☐	☐	☐	☐	☐	☐	☐	☐	☐	☐	☐	☐	☐	☐	☐	☐	☐	☐	☐	☐	☐
I offered my ideas to the group.	☐	☐	☐	☐	☐	☐	☐	☐	☐	☐	☐	☐	☐	☐	☐	☐	☐	☐	☐	☐	☐
I considered others' ideas carefully (even when they differed from mine).	☐	☐	☐	☐	☐	☐	☐	☐	☐	☐	☐	☐	☐	☐	☐	☐	☐	☐	☐	☐	☐
I worked as a team member.	☐	☐	☐	☐	☐	☐	☐	☐	☐	☐	☐	☐	☐	☐	☐	☐	☐	☐	☐	☐	☐
I created new materials.	☐	☐	☐	☐	☐	☐	☐	☐	☐	☐	☐	☐	☐	☐	☐	☐	☐	☐	☐	☐	☐
I helped solve a problem.	☐	☐	☐	☐	☐	☐	☐	☐	☐	☐	☐	☐	☐	☐	☐	☐	☐	☐	☐	☐	☐
Other observations and comments:																					

Daily Training Programme Evaluation Form

Date: _____

1. What were the major activities that you were involved in today? Please list what you can remember best.

_____

_____

_____

2. What proportion of today's activities do you think you directed as participants and what proportion was controlled by the facilitators?

_____

_____

_____

3. What was the most useful activity that was conducted today? Why?

_____

_____

_____

4. What did you learn from today's sessions? Please describe.

_____

_____

_____

5. What is your analysis of the training programme?
☐ Excellent   ☐ Good   ☐ Not very useful
Give your reasons for your choice.

_____

_____

_____

6. Comments on logistics — food, lodging, other physical arrangements.

_____

_____

_____

VI. FOLLOW-UP PLANNING: PUTTING PARTICIPATION INTO DAILY PRACTICE

A participatory training of trainers workshop is certainly not an end in itself. Ultimately, it aims to create the motivation and the competency needed by extension staff to bring about the full involvement of local communities, especially rural women, in their own work settings. It is also a means to promoting teamwork among field staff of different agencies covering the same or corresponding geographic areas or sharing common sectoral concerns. This calls for co-ordinated planning.

For this reason, towards the end of the workshop, close attention should be paid by the trainers to planning follow-up activities. This is done by focusing on three inter-related issues:

■ Which community education principles, methods and techniques introduced at the workshop are participants prepared to use in their own work upon their return to their respective agencies or project areas?

■ To what extent do participants feel ready to conduct similar participatory training of trainers activities on their own and, if so, when and how do they propose to do it?

■ What kind of support, and from what sources and levels, will participants need in order to do an effective job of involving local communities in development activities or programmes?

For example, in one workshop in preparation for the second of these tasks, participants were asked to divide themselves into homogenous groups by geographic location to design a three-day participatory workshop. In addition to its value as a planning activity, this exercise provided facilitators with important feedback: by requiring that the workshop design be limited to only three days, participants were obliged to be very selective as to activities they would choose from a large variety of options. This tested their ability to put together a condensed version of the workshop which still makes sense as a complete package. Their decisions on excluding or including items for a given target group measured their ability to adapt the process to different levels of sophistication of trainees or their time availability.

In another workshop, participants were divided into five functional groups according to their on-going responsibilities within the programme. Their task was to plan participatory activities that would be most appropriate for their local situation over a three-month period following the workshop.

Each group was asked to answer the following questions:

■ When you return to your work situation, how do you hope to use what you have learned in this workshop?

■ What resources do you already have to help you do this?

■ What other resources will you need?

■ Where can you obtain these resources? How?

In a third workshop, the teams were made up of extension workers from different sectors but grouped together according to the proximity of their duty stations. These teams were asked to consider how they would co-ordinate their activities in the field and ensure consistent use of the participatory approach.

The groups then involved themselves in the difficult task of defining educational programme plans for their own communities. They were asked to answer such questions as:

■ Which type of learning groups do you intend to form in your communities? How many and over what period of time?

■ How many sessions will be held, for what duration, and what will be the focus of the first phase of sessions?

■ Who will be responsible for each aspect of the programme?

■ How will materials be developed? What other techniques can you use which do not need visual materials?

In a fourth instance, participants used a technique called the "Impertinent Pert Chart" (See the *Methods/Planning* Activities in Part II). This technique requires the listing of all of the steps needed to achieve an objective in a given period of time — in this case, to ensure that the WSS programme involves the community to the maximum degree.

Planning of the steps to be taken was done in streams assigned to subgroups according to their special interest, such as training, materials development, hardware, administration, among others. These streams were then compared, adjusted and synchronised in a time frame.

To ensure that plans developed by participants do not remain paper plans, group members are asked to make a personal commitment, individually, to get to one or more steps — however small — immediately upon returning to their sponsoring agencies.

Reports on follow-up to PROWWESS country workshops are extremely encouraging, indicating that enthusiasm continues to be high and that the principles learned are being widely used. There is, however, a scarcity of training materials and participatory learning aids. The gap is serious enough to be considered a con-

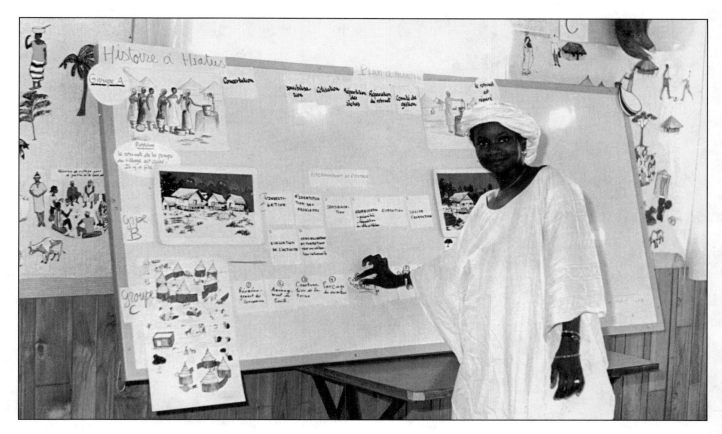

straint to expanding the approach on a national scale. This is a problem which PROWWESS is seeking to address through its regional-level dialogues with trainers.

What kind of support is needed for this mainstreaming to happen? It is generally agreed that the achievement of most follow-up projections would depend on interest and support at the provincial level and higher up. Project managers, administrators, and policymakers must be convinced that participatory training is a good investment. Only then will such training have a permanent place in the project cycle. The promotion of the idea of community participation and in particular of women's involvement is thus a task that needs priority attention at all levels.

Because of the urgency of convincing higher level decision-makers about the value of participatory approaches throughout the entire programme, a special invitation is generally issued at all PROWWESS workshops to key people to attend the final session. At this time, the participants are in the best position to recount, from their own experience, what the benefits of the process are and what support is needed to make these benefits last.

The pride of ownership with which participants describe the happenings and products of the workshop is in itself a testimony to the participatory process. It is akin to the pride with which local communities may be expected to speak of the local project activities in which they have made a personal investment.

PART II

39 PARTICIPATORY TRAINING ACTIVITIES

I. NOTES TO THE TRAINER ON SELECTING AND SEQUENCING ACTIVITIES

Part I of this manual presented background on the SARAR process as utilised and further developed by PROWWESS in promoting community participation. Part II is a collection of training activities, the building blocks you can use for your own training programme.

The activities are grouped under four main categories: HUMAN DEVELOPMENT, METHODS, FIELD REALITY and THEORY.

The categories correspond to four central aims of a training of trainers workshop: to use group process in a way that leads to human development, to introduce trainers to new methods, to make training relevant by basing it on participants' own reality and to draw out theory from this lived experience.

The METHODS category is most emphasised because mastery of new participatory methods liberates participants from less effective teaching practices and helps them approach reality-based needs in a more dynamic way. METHODS are subdivided into five areas, which correspond to the flow of activities in a particular training programme: **creative, investigative, analytic, planning** and **informative.**

The overall workshop sequence interweaves activities from the four categories, so that each activity builds on the learning that precedes it. Any training programme will be different, depending on the mix of participants and objectives to be achieved. Generally, however, programmes follow the sequence depicted in the chart on the next page.

Sample Participatory Training Workshop Flow Agenda

Monday	Tuesday	Wednesday	Thursday	Friday	Saturday	Sunday	Monday	Tuesday	Wednesday
	Human Development		Planning Methods		Preparation of village learning experience	OPEN	Village learning experience	Follow-up planning	Closing ceremony
	Creative Methods								
	Investigative Methods		Information Methods						
Field Reality									
Field Visit			Field Reality						
		Analytical Methods							
		Field Reality					Feedback on village learning experience	Workshop evaluation	
Theory (as needed) →									
Evaluation /Documentation →									→

You will find that all of the activities in the manual have elements that correspond to all four major categories. They have been clustered in these categories to make the job of designing a workshop easier. Once you use the activities and become familiar with them, you might want to assess the activities from your own experience. The "Overall Design Review Grid", presented in Part I in the evaluation section on page 46, is a useful tool for examining the emphases and balance of the activities in your programme.

To start selecting your workshop activities you may begin by deciding whether your trainees need to focus on a practical real life problem (Field Reality) such as the extension worker's workload or the role of women in the sector, or whether they need reinforcement in a particular concept or principle (Theory) such as the importance of open communication or the need to understand different types of resistance to change.

Having decided on your primary focus related to *Field Reality* or *Theory*, you would then need to consider what *Methods* and *Human Development* processes would help you to involve your trainees most effectively.

Please keep in mind that THEORY, as such, is the least emphasised content area since the aim is to help participants arrive at theory on their own through analysis of the activity in which they have been involved.

Before turning to the specific activities on pages 69 - 172, it is important that you carefully review the explanation of rationale and approach on the following pages for all four main categories and their components; you will then see more clearly what purpose each activity fulfils and how it can be integrated into a larger framework. As said earlier, without this type of insight the exercises themselves may end up as a "bag of tricks" which can dazzle but confuse trainees rather than help them to grow. The descriptions of the four categories also include an index of the activities which are most closely related to each category. This can serve as an invaluable guide for selecting the activities.

II. CATEGORIES OF TRAINING ACTIVITIES

Human Development

A vital difference between participatory and didactic training is the emphasis that is placed on establishing horizontal relationships and maintaining a cordial atmosphere throughout a participatory workshop. The activities you introduce must be such that participants begin to see each other as a resource and to understand that good teamwork requires recognising the contribution each member can make.

The team building process begins on Day One. It is up to you to create a climate of trust and mutual respect. If participants are respected for their experience, ideas, and potential, they will be more likely to participate actively in generating fresh ideas.

The activities in this category include useful exercises for starting your programme as well as those you can use later as tension breakers or as means to strengthen group interaction. The activities will enable your participants to:

- express their expectations of the workshop;

- build peer relationships;

- develop skills in working in a group;

- and appreciate their abilities and those of other group members.

Some of the activities can also serve to integrate participants from different backgrounds, such as village people, trainers, and technical experts. In these groups, it is important to break down hierarchies among the participants, include everyone in discussion, and assess different perspectives and kinds of capabilities.

Your ongoing feedback sessions and evaluation exercises are another invaluable way to strengthen the participatory group process. The sample evaluation tools in Part I (pp. 45 - 50) are the kinds of feedback mechanisms that need to be used on a daily basis in your programme.

Here is a list of the Human Development activities, with brief descriptions and page numbers of the complete activities.

Methods

Methods are the core of a SARAR workshop. These are the tools that will enable your participant trainers to create effective learning experiences at the village level for enabling villagers to conceptualise and carry our specific projects. METHODS are organised in five clusters and are sequenced to have a cumulative effect. First, participants are involved in using their *creativity* and at looking at situations in new ways. Then, they gain tools for *investigating* and *analysing* their reality. Finally, they develop skills in *planning* and *accessing information* for water and sanitation or other community development initiatives.

Here is more information on the clusters of Methods and lists of activities for each cluster:

Creative Methods

In the final analysis, the major transformation in village living conditions which we hope for, will depend not so much on how many good ideas we generate for the people, but on how open villagers themselves are to innovation, how imaginatively they look at their resources and how ingeniously they go about resolving their problems. Helping villagers to use their imaginative faculties thus becomes a legitimate and urgent goal of community education.

Unlocking creativity is given the highest priority in the SARAR approach to training. PROWWESS shares in the belief that each individual has enormous reserves of energy and talent that remain undiscovered and untapped. Creativity is part of a vast unexplored reserve of power available for development at the community level, yet too few development programmes acknowledge it, much less capitalise on it. These activities will enable you to do so in your programme:

Investigative Methods

These activities enable villagers to do their own needs assessment by collecting and compiling data on problems and situations in their own locale. In many development efforts, academicians or technical experts are the ones who gather and analyse information while the people are marginally involved. Village-level participation in this phase is vital; it enables community members themselves to gain a fuller understanding of their problems and to contribute their insights on causes and alternative solutions.

The following activities will involve your participants in finding out more about their situation:

Analytic Methods

The analysis cluster of activities is designed to enable your participants to examine a problem in depth, so that they can better understand its causes and identify alternative ways of solving it.

In the SARAR workshop sequence, analytic methods follow rather than precede creative exercises. The assumption is that analysis or the use of judgement (e.g. probing, sorting, classifying, interpreting) calls for exactness, precision, objectivity and logic. While creative exercises help people to look at their environment imaginatively, analytic activities help them to identify the most logical and efficient procedures to arrive at solutions, and to define the needs for personnel, funds or equipment.

Thus both functions are vital, but must be introduced in a way that does not sacrifice one for the other. If analysis takes place too early, every new idea could be shot down by premature judgement and people would hesitate to make suggestions out of fear of criticism. After creativity has had its chance, analysis and evaluation can and should take over to select the best ideas for implementation.

If you introduce a series of analytic exercises in your training programme, it will help your trainees (and they in turn will help villagers) to use critical thinking skills in daily life. Thus, they will be better prepared for a partnership role in development through repeated practice in making group decisions based on objective assessment, careful analysis and sound judgement.

Among the many activities that can help trainees learn analytic skills are the following:

Planning Methods

The involvement of local communities in development activities requires a certain minimum ability to plan. This applies in particular to water sector activities where the collaboration of local people in achieving programme targets on schedule is expected. To this end, community members, including women, will need to serve on water committees, raise funds, decide who is to be trained for which task, and when and how they will be compensated.

Average villagers are not used to community-level planning of programmes. They often entrust planning decisions to prestigious leaders and other authority figures. Such decision-making is an especially unaccustomed role for village women.

How does one simplify the planning process sufficiently to be understandable by all? Which kinds of educational opportunities can provide experience and practice in the use of basic planning skills?

The following planning activities include varying levels of complexity:

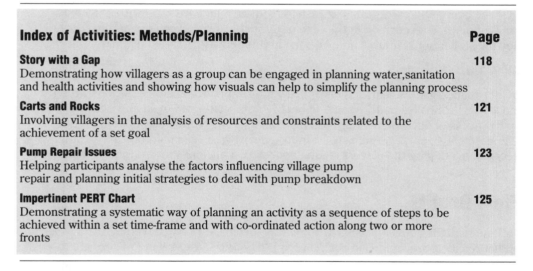

Informative Methods

In all of the above activities, participants will feel the need for information and eagerly seek it out. At this point, didactic teaching materials may be appropriate. However, they will be able to master the content faster and retain information better if the session involves their participation in some way.

As a trainer, the way you carry out activities will be as important as the selection of the activities themselves. Here are some kinds of activities that will help you to impart information in a participatory way.

Demonstrations

Demonstrations can be more effective when the learner has an active role and does not merely observe the trainer. For example, in a workshop in Kenya, participants accompanied the Pump Installation Team to two repair sites where they helped in the demonstration of removing a pump from a bore hole, partial dismantlement, reassembly and installation.

Contests

Learners can form teams to gather information and apply it to solve problems in competition. For example, correctly naming different parts of a pump or the nutritional value of different foods.

Needs Assessment Brainstorming

This is a technique in which learners actively define what they want to learn and when and how. For example, the community women and the trainers might list all the pump-related questions that still needed answers. Then the resource person comes in and provides the exact information that the participants want.

Information-sharing Exercises

Participants begin by reviewing what they already know about a subject and talk with their peers and specialists about filling the gaps.

Evaluative Exercises

In these exercises, participants are asked to identify and order priorities, such as ranking diseases according to the ease or difficulty of securing community coopera-tion for prevention. Pictures may be used in this activity.

Informative Games

In informative games, learning takes place not simply from chance right or wrong moves, as in "Snakes and Ladders" (a board game often used by health educators), but by a process of decision-making leading to a goal. The "SARAR Sanitation Health Game Activity", p. 127, demonstrates how a board game can combine information with decision-making by the players so that information becomes meaningful to them.

Field Reality

Although all the activities focus in some way on village reality, several critical aspects of that reality arose again and again in the PROWWESS experience. There are three areas which we believe need to be highlighted as a means to enhance programme effectiveness, and each is described below.

Community Participation from Various Perspectives: People who come to your work-shop will bring different concepts of community participation and different experi-ences with it in the past. An examination of these varying views is usually scheduled early on in the workshop, so that a common foundation of understanding can be created. This is particularly the case in groups that include a mix of extension workers and technical specialists or people from different job levels within a Ministry.

The Situation of Rural Women: The involvement of rural women in development activities is particularly difficult to achieve for two reasons: their daily chores leave them little or no time of their own and they have often been culturally secluded from public life.

The majority of rural women have had no experience in community-level decision-making. In addition to poverty, illiteracy, ill-health and overwork, rural women are hampered by a whole range of psycho-social barriers to participation. Many of these factors tend to be ignored because they are intangibles. They include:

- feelings of dependency

- low self-esteem

- fear of disapproval of husbands or elders

- lack of awareness of common purposes and resources

- inability to take economic risks

- fear of tasks that require unfamiliar skills or that may increase their workload.

It is important that extension workers be fully aware of the dimensions of the problem but they must reach this understanding through problem-posing activities, not by didactic methods.

Workshop participants must also become aware that the situation of women has to be addressed in an integrated way. Piecemeal solutions, such as simply bringing water closer to home, are by themselves not enough.

The training of women must also address issues of personal growth and of group strength as priorities. Women need assistance to experience success, to feel differently and more positively about themselves, and to gain credibility in the eyes of the community.

In this light, the participatory approach to women's training makes good sense because it focuses on human development and group process, combined with practical goals that the women set for themselves.

The Roles and Responsibilities of Extension Agents and Technical Experts: In the beginning, PROWWESS workshops were directed toward "software" personnel, such as health education and community development officers. However, the good intentions of a software person are often frustrated upon colliding with "hardware" targets and technicalities; hence the need for joint training of multi-sectoral staff.

In an integrated training programme, it is best to encourage a merger of interests right from the start and to sustain it throughout the programme. This can be done by integrating a small number of hardware personnel in each subgroup where they can establish close dialogue with software specialists.

The fact that group members function as a team to complete a task helps to unify the interests and inputs of the members regardless of professional orientation. Also, it is helpful to enable field workers to examine their jobs in terms of tasks and time involved, so that realistic workplans can be developed.

Your Own Key Reality Issues: In your workshop or workshops, you may come across field reality issues that are important in your own situation. When this occurs, do not feel limited by the activities in this manual. Rather, use the activities as prototypes for creating your own exercises on your own key issues.

The following activities are useful for exploring field realities:

Theory

Very little theory as such is actually taught in the workshop sessions. Rather, participants are helped to arrive at theory on their own, as far as possible, through the analysis of experience and by discussing the structure, process, and outputs of workshop activities. Practical insights developed in this way are then linked to more general theoretical frameworks.

The frameworks we have found most useful relate to: principles of community participation; aspects of adult learning; the process of change; and interpersonal communication.

You can draw theory from the following activities as needed in your workshop programme:

III. DESCRIPTIONS OF THE TRAINING ACTIVITIES
(in categorical order)

BASELINE ATTITUDINAL ASSESSMENT

PURPOSE:

To assess participants' openness to taking initiative, to being creative, becoming involved in group work and problem-solving.

TIME: 20-30 minutes

MATERIALS:

Copy of the form for each participant.

NOTE TO TRAINER:

The form provides a baseline assessment to compare with a similar questionnaire later in the workshop. Those who rate themselves as being more reserved or less articulate at the start generally end up showing considerable improvement in their group work skills and in their readiness to take on active roles. The trainers can use this exercise later with extension workers.

This initial assessment must take place at the time of registration, before participants have had exposure to any group activities including introductions. You can adapt this form to your own purposes but be sure to include items on which you expect to see some attitudinal or behavioural growth.

PROCEDURES:

■ Before distributing the form, ask participants to choose a symbol by which they would each identify their form at a later stage without the need to write their names. This is in the interest of confidentiality.

■ When a similar form is distributed at mid-point or towards the end of the work-shop they should use the same symbol so that the two forms can be matched and note taken of any changes which may have occurred in the interim period.

FORM

How I tend to behave:

Check one.

In a group discussion I generally

☐   lead the discussion.

☐   take an active role but not necessarily a lead role.

☐   prefer to sit and listen.

SYMBOL

In dealing with village people or trainees in my field, I usually use the following method(s):

List up to three in order of most frequent use.

_____

_____

If invited to act in a role play or socio-drama, I generally:

Check one.

☐   am a bit uncertain but willing to try.

☐   prefer to stay out and watch.

☐   feel role playing is a waste of time.

If asked to draw a picture, I generally:

Check one.

☐   am moderately confident.

☐   feel unsure but willing to try.

☐   am convinced I cannot draw and prefer to leave it to others.

☐   believe drawing is pointless in a workshop.

EXPRESSING HOPES AND FEARS

PURPOSE:

To share expectations, hopes and fears about the workshop that can be monitored during the training.

TIME: 20-30 minutes

MATERIALS:

Newsprint, two blank cards or sheets of paper for each participant. Tape or tacks for the wall.

NOTE TO TRAINER:

This exercise demonstrates to the participants on the first day that the trainer values their opinions and will be open to constructive criticism. Also, participants can find support for their hopes and reassurance on their fears through group discussion, which is an important step towards building confidence. The exercise can later be used with extension workers.

Most workshops begin by asking participants what they expect from the workshops, but if the expectations are not written down, they may be forgotten and serve little constructive purpose. This written exercise can also encourage communication on issues beyond the training programme, such as concerns about family while attending the programme.

PROCEDURES:

■ Have participants sit in three small groups of not more than ten persons each.

- Distribute two strips of paper per participant.

- Ask participants to write their hopes and fears about the outcomes of the work-shop on the two small strips of paper. This is to be done individually, without consultation.

- Ask each small group to share among themselves what they have written.

- Ask participants to post Hopes and Fears on the wall in separate sections and then to read each other's lists.

- In a large group discussion, ask analytical questions about the list, such as "What strikes you most about these?"

- Remind participants during the programme to check periodically if their hopes have been fulfilled and fears overcome.

Here are some examples of hopes and fears expressed by participants at a PROWWESS Regional Participatory Training Workshop held in Tanzania:

Hopes

To share experience

To learn more about the SARAR method

To make new friends

To become better trainers

To learn more ways of mobilising rural women

To develop facilitating skills

To design, pretest and evaluate training materials

To learn more about how to truly reach and involve the grassroots people

To determine the suitability of participatory techniques

in different countries and cultural contexts in Africa

To go on field trips and study tours

To learn more about the achievements and failures of different training initiatives in Africa

Fears

The workshop may fail to achieve all its objectives

It might involve too much work

The themes may not be well grasped

It might not be useful due to participants' inexperience with such methods

Emphasis on women's role may not be sufficient

All participants may not be fully involved

The reaction of the villagers may not be positive

Methods may seem too childish to adult villagers

Follow-up evaluation may not take place

Language may prove a barrier

This activity was introduced to PROWWESS by Jane Vella, Consultant.

GROUP SELF-SELECTION

PURPOSE:

To give participants maximum possible scope to choose the groups in which they would like to work so as to ensure their sense of belonging in the group.

TIME: 30 minutes

MATERIALS:

Three large labels A, B and C (or other names).

Colour-coded name tags for all participants to indicate their professional field (e.g. hardware/software) and function (e.g. trainer, supervisor, extension worker, village volunteer).

NOTE TO TRAINER:

This exercise demonstrates how the facilitator, by giving up control, can stimulate an increased sense of responsibility and autonomy among participants. It also sets up groups in which participants will function for the greater part of the training programme.

While participants will work in these groups most of the time, they will have an opportunity to form other small groups, usually much smaller, later in the programme.

PROCEDURES:

■ Post the three labels A, B and C as group names on the blackboard not too close together. Allow space for participants to mill around while they decide under which label they wish to pin their names.

■ Invite participants to pin name tags under any one of these group headings only making sure that:

Each group has no more than one-third the total number of participants.

There is equal (or near equal) distribution of participants by gender, work function, specialisation or other variables.

■ If any one of the groups seems unbalanced, ask participants: "Could you please check whether all three groups are well balanced? If not, please make the necessary changes in name tags yourselves until you are satisfied that the groups match." They should voluntarily move their name tags to other groups, trading places with those who would, by so doing, also help to balance out the groups.

■ When the self-selection process is complete, ask the three groups to sit at different tables and to write down the names of their group members on newsprint. They should also select a chairperson and rapporteur for their group; these roles could be filled on a rotating basis if they wish.

PERSONAL ADJECTIVES

PURPOSE:

To introduce participants to each other in an enjoyable way. This exercise helps people to learn about each other in an informal way that builds group spirit.

TIME: 20-30 minutes

MATERIALS:

None.

PROCEDURES:

■ Ask each participant to think of an adjective which corresponds to the first letter of his or her first name.

■ Have participants sit in a circle.

■ Beginning anywhere, have one participant introduce him/herself saying "My name is ...... My adjective is ......" or "I am (adjective) (first name)".

■ The next participant then introduces him/herself in the same way and repeats the name and adjective of the preceding person. The process is repeated around the circle, each one in turn having to remember the names and adjectives of all the participants who have introduced themselves in the order in which they are seated.

Introduced by the national core team members at a PROWWESS-assisted workshop in Zimbabwe.

GROUP DYNAMICS

PURPOSE:

To relax or recharge the group after a particularly intensive intellectual activity or at the start of the afternoon session.

TIME: Under 15 minutes

MATERIALS:

Paper. See each activity below.

NOTE TO TRAINER:

These quick exercises break tension and give new energy to the group, especially at times when they are slow to begin or have finished a difficult intellectual task.

These are various short exercises from which you can choose.

PERCENTAGE OF AGREEMENT

■ On the walls in four different parts of the room place signs indicating percentages as follows: 0, 25%, 50%, 75%, 100%.

■ Make a list of six to eight controversial statements such as "Physical Punishment for Children", "Nuclear Weapons", "Divorce", "Men Fetching Water", "Ban on Smoking", "Didactic Teaching", "Education for Village Girls", or "Death Penalty for Drug Peddlers". Make up your own statements according to the local culture, but be careful to choose statements on which the participants will feel comfortable in taking a public stand.

■ Ask the participants to decide to what extent they agree or disagree with each statement that is called out. They should then move to that part of the room which has a percent sign which most closely reflects their position on the issue.

■ The composition of groups under each sign will naturally change with the different issues addressed. If you want to extend the exercise, you can ask each group to discuss their reasons.

WHO IS THE LEADER?

Have participants sit in a circle. Ask for a volunteer who will leave the room and return only when called. Upon returning the volunteer must guess who is the leader of the group.

While the volunteer is out, invite any one group member to act as the leader while two others at two different parts of the circle act as "mirrors". The leader's job is to start some action (such as clapping) and keep it going rhythmically for a few moments, then change to another action (such as stamping with one foot) and again, after a few seconds, to yet another. The "mirrors" should discreetly watch the leader and copy the movements without letting the volunteer notice that they are "copying" and not "initiating." The rest of the group should get their cues by looking at the "mirrors", rather than at the leader so as to confuse the volunteer.

After the group has done a few movements, the volunteer should try to guess which person in the circle has acted as the leader for that round of the game.

THE VIRUS CARRIER

Cut and fold as many pieces of paper (about one inch [2.54 cm] square) as there are participants. Leave all blank except one, which should have the words "virus carrier" written on it. Fold them carefully and pass them out for participants to pick as in a lottery.

People should look at the papers they have picked without permitting others to see them. (This applies to the "virus carrier" in particular.)

Participants then mill around the room looking at each other as they do so. The virus carrier must try to catch someone's eye and wink. That person then is supposed to have caught the virus and must fall to the ground or stagger out of the crowd taking one or two other persons along (whomever the infected person touches while collapsing). All these people must leave the game as soon as infected but should not disclose who infected them.

The game goes on till participants guess who is the virus carrier before the latter has had a chance to wink at them.

THE HOT POTATO

Roll up newspaper into a ball and make it larger by adding several other layers of newspaper. Between each layer insert a piece of paper on which a forfeit or penalty is written.

Have participants sit in a circle and pass the "ball" quickly from one person to the next clockwise. Play music on a tape recorder. One member of the facilitator team should sit facing away from the group and turn off the music at will.

As soon as the music stops, the person who has the ball must open one layer of newspaper, read the penalty and perform it. The music and the passing of the ball are then resumed. If preferred, the penalties can be performed later after they have all been disclosed.

BIG FISH/LITTLE FISH

Have participants stand in a circle.

The facilitator (or assistant) should stand in the middle facing different participants by turns. When the facilitator calls out "Big Fish" he or she must use gestures which stand for the opposite, a little fish.

The person facing the facilitator must respond by saying "Little Fish" but using the gesture for Big Fish. To increase the suspense, the facilitator changes frequently from Big Fish to Little Fish and tries to catch different group members when they are least prepared.

Any group member who responds incorrectly either verbally or by gesture has to drop out of the game.

COMMUNITY OF FIVE

Ask participants to stand in groups of five at the start of this activity.

Tell them you are going to call out different numbers and accordingly, they should break up their groups and make new groups of a size matching the number you call. You may call out "three," for example, then "six", "four", "two" and maybe "five" again.

Each time participants have to make quick decisions as to whom to join or whom to let go or exclude. Those who are not in groups corresponding in size to the number you called out have to drop out of the game at that point.

At the conclusion of this game, you could open a discussion of how the participants felt about belonging to or being left out of groups. The similarity to community affiliations and factions could then be explored.

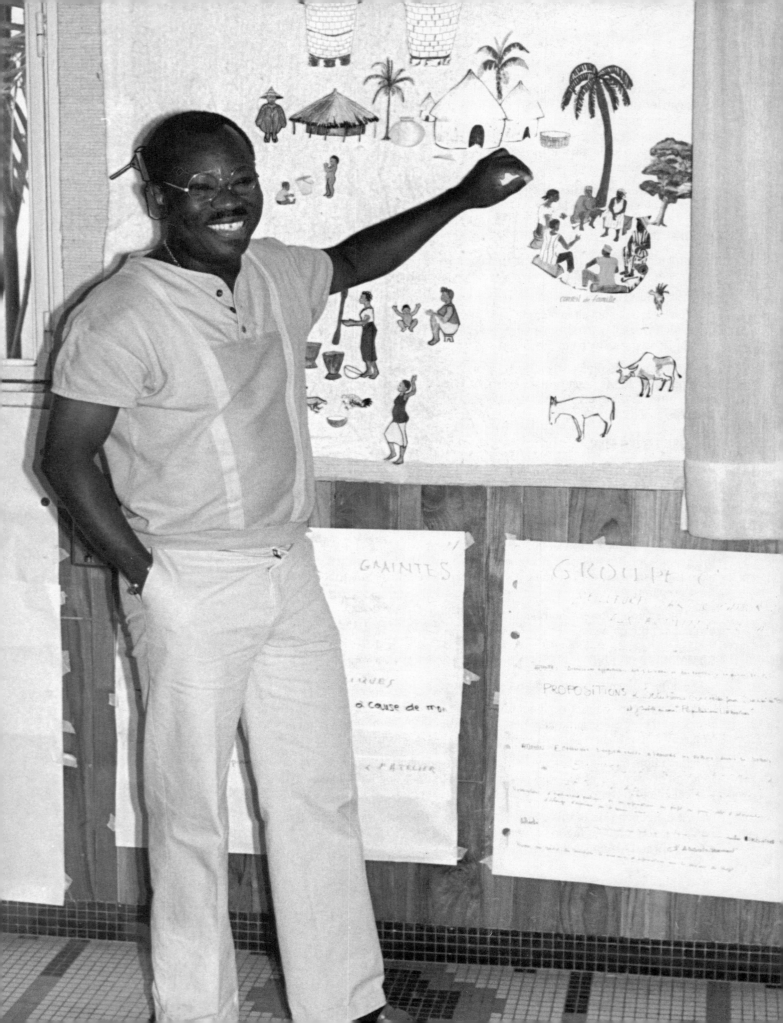

FLEXI-FLANS
AS CREATIVE MATERIALS

PURPOSE:

To demonstrate how materials such as flexi-flans can be used to increase the creative participation of the learner.

To illustrate the range of creative responses that can be expected from the use of open-ended materials such as flexis.

To reinforce the group's understanding of the difference between learner-centred and didactic or directive training methods.

TIME: 30-40 minutes

MATERIALS:

A wide variety of flexi-flans and a flannel board on which to arrange them. It is important that the human figures be of people of different ages, both male and female, and represent different socio-economic backgrounds. They should also be facing in different directions (e.g. front view and left/right profile) so that they can be arranged to represent two or more people engaged in a conversation or discussion. (See samples on the following pages).

Flexi-flans consist of paper cut-outs of human figures with flexible arms, legs and torsos which can be placed on a flannel-covered board to illustrate a point of view or to relate an incident or a story. In addition to the human figures, a number of props are included in the set (houses, trees, animals, tools, vehicles). A large variety of figures and props will stimulate participants to select, combine and compose scenarios of their own. In making flexi-flans, popularly known as "flexis", it is preferable to use heavy paper or very light cardboard which is stiff enough to retain shape, but not so heavy as to be difficult to punch through the double thickness where arms and legs are to be joined to the torso.

NOTE TO TRAINER:

This exercise introduces participants to the use of open-ended materials, which can be used in many training settings.

You and your trainers will need to make your own flexi-flan figures and props, so allow sufficient time to prepare for this exercise. If you have the help of an artist, he or she should start designing flexis as soon as possible, since quantity and variety are important. Participants should help in colouring, cutting, assembling on a mass production basis.

Flexis can be a powerful and creative communication tool in learner-centred training, especially when working with a group which includes illiterates. Participants should be strongly encouraged to use them as a way of drawing out ideas from the group and as a method of starting discussions, not as a tool to "teach" messages to the trainees or villagers. To use flexis for didactic purposes may confuse the participants and inhibit them from freely using the material on their own and as their own.

PROCEDURES:

■ Introduce flexi-flans as a communication tool similar in function to the alphabet. The flexi figures can be combined in innumerable ways to express ideas, feelings, events, hopes and concerns, in the same way that letters can be combined into words to express thought and emotion, experiences and plans.

■ Propose a simple task using minimal instructions, such as suggesting that the participants use the flexis to share something about themselves or their community or an event that they recall with pride or amusement.

■ Plan how you are going to state the task so that your instructions are brief, to the point, and clear. Impress on them that their creativity is what matters. Allow at least 30 minutes for this task.

■ Have the groups share their creativity at a plenary session.

Sample Flexi Flans

Sample Flexi Flans

Sample Flexi Flans

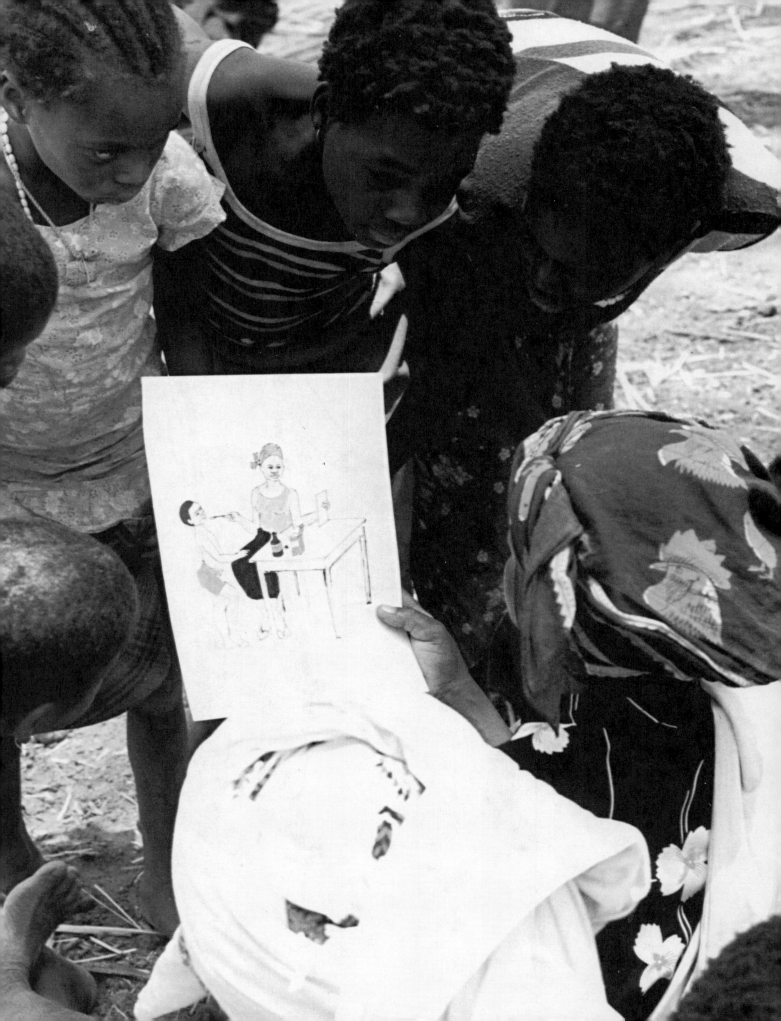

UNSERIALISED POSTERS

PURPOSE:

To demonstrate how open-ended and flexible visual aids encourage creativity and how they provide a tool to stimulate discussion of important real life issues among participants.

TIME: 40-50 minutes

MATERIALS:

Three copies of a set of 10 to 15 pictures or "posters" (roughly 8 1/2 x 11 inches or 210 x 297 mm), each depicting a dramatic human situation such as a dispute between two people, a heated group meeting, a young boy chasing or being chased down the street, a family in trouble, an illness, a community festivity, or an individual deep in reflection.

These scenes are represented in such a way that they are open to many different interpretations. The facilitator who prepares this material should not have any one story line in mind. Since these posters are "un"-serialised, i.e. they are not numbered in any set order, participants can rearrange them in any sequence they choose.

NOTE TO TRAINER:

This exercise reinforces the idea that neutral, open-ended visual aids can be important tools for trainers in participatory training programmes. Used in a village setting, the facilitators can learn much about the community from the stories created and the discussion of issues.

The success of the exercise rests in a major way on the selection of the pictures. They should be truly evocative, depict dramatic human scenes and be widely open to

Sample Unserialised Posters

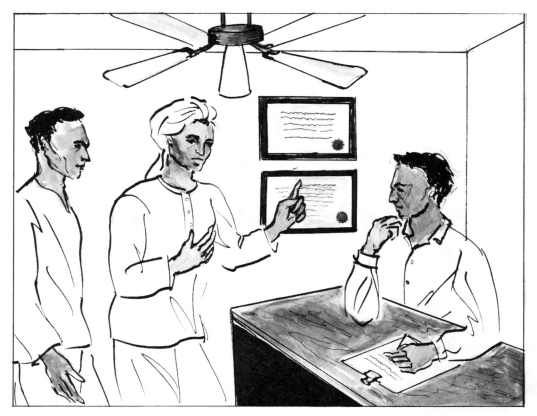

Sample Unserialised Posters

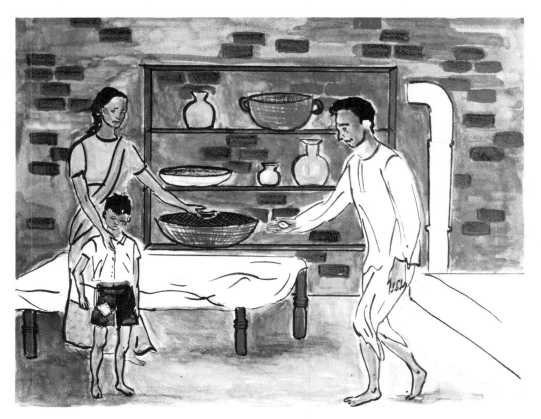

interpretation. Simply putting together a set of pictures from assorted magazines or other sources will not assure the desired results. The themes should not be biased by the professional focus of the workshop. In particular, if the set includes pictures which have a clear-cut sectoral message (such as nutrition, family planning or health), the stories may all tend to focus on that message, on the assumption that it is the "right answer" expected by the facilitators. The activity then ceases to be truly creative and we learn little from it.

If pictures cannot be obtained, you can explain the exercise and ask trainers to draw a picture of a dramatic episode in their own lives. They can use stick figures, symbols or other aids. This method allows the trainers to see a variety of ideas and themes which they can then translate into large poster pictures for use in the villages.

You may find that the groups choose similar pictures but compose quite different stories from them; or they may choose different pictures but the stories may turn out to be similar. The reasons for differences or similarities in the stories should be thoroughly analysed by the group.

When done at the village level, villagers may be surprised and elated to find that their stories could yield a long and impressive list of issues for further discussion.

PROCEDURES:

■ Divide the participants into three groups. Give each group a copy of the full set of posters.

■ Instruct them to choose any four posters out of their set and weave them into a story giving names to the characters and to the community or village context in which the story takes place. Remind them that the story should have a plot with a beginning, a middle, and an ending. Allow 15 to 20 minutes for this task.

■ When all groups are ready, invite them to tell their stories in a plenary session using the posters to illustrate the sequence of events.

■ Have one member of each group note down the key issues and themes that have surfaced from the discussion of their story. Let participants as a whole reflect on how the issues and themes noted could serve as the basis for other learner-centred activities.

POCKET CHART

PURPOSE:

To demonstrate a tool that will help villagers learn a new way to assess and analyse their situation.

TIME: 1 hour

MATERIALS:

The Pocket Chart, in its simplest form consists of rows of pockets, usually four to six horizontally and six to ten vertically. A set of pictures is attached above the top row of pockets. These pictures represent areas in which data are needed, such as different sources of domestic water supply (river, pond, uncovered well, pump). Each of these pictures is placed at the head of a vertical column. (If desired, pictures can also be attached down the left-hand side to indicate other variables, such as different population groups of men, women, children or income or social subsets who use the options.)

If a Pocket Chart is not available, trainers can use other containers, such as earthen pots, into which people can place their votes.

Slips of Paper for voting for use by volunteers.

NOTE TO TRAINER:

This activity exposes trainers to a tool which they can adapt for their own work. It demonstrates that it is both easy and valuable to familiarise average village people with simple data collection procedures.

The Pocket Chart is an investigative tool that enables villagers to carry out data collection, tabulation, and analysis on their own. It can then help them analyse their needs and priorities.

When using the Pocket Chart with villagers in a group meeting, six to ten volunteers may each be given a voting slip or some substitute item to be placed in pockets in the top row to indicate which options the volunteer's family normally utilises. To observe confidentiality, the Chart may be placed facing away from the audience and the volunteers go single file to deposit their votes.

This activity can be made more complex by asking more than one question and using more than one type of voting slip. For example, if we wanted to know which water sources are occasionally used, as opposed to normally used, we could provide voting slips of two different colours.

The level of complexity and sophistication can be further increased by attaching pictures down the left-hand margin of the pocket chart to represent different purposes for which the water is used in the family. You could then ask participants: "For each purpose, from which source do you usually draw water?"

The voting part of the activity should be done as quickly as possible to retain the interest of the other participants. Since many will remain passive while the volunteers are voting, the trainer should be prepared with ideas of how to keep the non-voters busy.

In case there are many votes in certain pockets, the trainer should have a separate strip of paper or tape to attach the votes in a vertical row.

While some participants are tabulating the results, the rest of the group needs to see what is going on and to be a part of the process of reflecting on the information. Their comments should be carefully noted.

By changing the pictures, the same Pocket Charts can be used for other themes, such as rural sanitation, nutrition, income producing activities, health practices or common ailments.

Beyond this exercise, the Pocket Chart can be used for a variety of training purposes, such as to compare and evaluate different activities, to assess the achievement of specific objectives or to vote on priorities. In some workshops, we have also used an adaptation of the Pocket Chart to determine to what extent the participants' original fears have been overcome and hopes met through the workshop process.

PROCEDURES:

■ Explain to the group how the pocket chart can be used to provide data on current practices which are illustrated in the top horizontal row of pictures.

■ Invite some 5 or 6 volunteers to role play as villagers. Ask them to take one voting slip (or substitute item) each. This voting disc is to be placed in the pocket corresponding to the option which the villager normally uses.

■ Invite their suggestions on how the voting can be kept confidential and how to avoid voters being influenced by seeing how others have voted ahead of them. (One suggestion may be to turn the board on which the chart has been placed, so as to face away from the audience).

■ When confidentiality has been assured, let participant "volunteers" begin voting, one by one.

■ At the end of voting, invite another set of volunteers to remove the votes carefully from each pocket in full view of the audience, and to "tabulate" them, i.e. attach them to the pocket in a way that is easy for all to count the discs. This can be done, for example, with the help of a strip of paper to which the votes for that pocket can be attached.

■ When tabulation has been completed, the group should reflect on what the data generated means to them e.g. "Why do so many (or so few) people avail of this (or that) option? Is this sample representative of most people in our village? If not, what other options do other people prefer? What is the effect of these choices on their health or well-being?"

■ Practical implications for future behaviour should then be discussed.

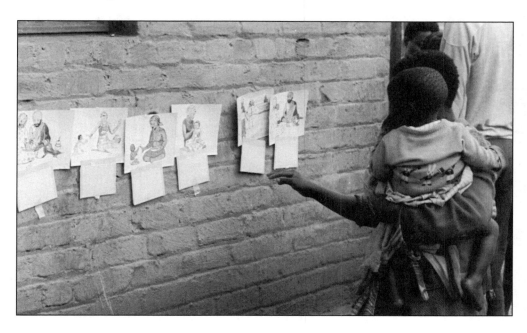

Pocket Chart Sample Pictures

Water Sources

Pocket Chart Sample Pictures
Water Uses

MAP BUILDING

PURPOSE:

To gather information about a community and its issues by having participants create their own map.

TIME: 2-3 hours

MATERIALS:

Newsprint, markers, all kinds of scrap materials such as cotton balls, thread, pebbles, shells, twigs, buttons, saw dust, clay, whatever is available. Divide these into three identical lots. Keep the materials where the map will be built.

NOTE TO TRAINER:

This exercise provides a tool that can be used by trainers and extension workers at the village level. It is especially useful in gathering information about a community and in planning activities. Again, the activity for the trainers reinforces the idea that participants play a major role in a successful participatory exercise.

This activity is exciting though time-consuming. If participants are not able to complete their maps within an hour or two, they could continue during leisure hours or on the following day. Because such valuable information and insights come out of this activity, it should not be rushed.

If scrap material is not easily available, the same map activity can be done as a drawing exercise, using newsprint and coloured markers.

One variation when the exercise is used with trainers is this: Ask everyone to work on the map from the point of view of villagers, except for two people who can add details or highlights from an outsider's perspective. In a mixed group, you could ask some to work on it from the perspectives of men and women.

PROCEDURES:

■ Have the trainers work in three groups, each around a table or other work surface. Invite them to discuss what a typical village community might look like and to plan its layout. They can then use the scrap material to create a three-dimensional map based on their plan. Participants are allowed to add other scrap materials if they wish. The group should give their village a name and note its size, population and other basic information.

■ While building the map, group members should write down a descriptive statement of their village on large newsprint that represents a profile of the village.

■ When all three maps have been completed, the participants should take each other on a "village tour" where they are briefed on each village map. Besides explaining the topography of the village, its lay-out, and demographic distribution, the briefing should describe the lives of the people there; what things they are proud of, and what are seen by them as problems.

■ Ask the groups to discuss and report on how this exercise could be used or adapted for use by villagers and as an entry point for discussion of specific issues such as water supply or women's development.

THREE-PILE SORTING CARDS

PURPOSE:

To develop analytical and problem-solving skills and the ability to reflect on causes and effects.

To get to know the extent to which participants are fully aware of the positive or negative implications of a variety of situations shown to them.

TIME: 30-45 minutes

MATERIALS:

A set of some 9 to 15 cards, each with a picture of a scene which could be interpreted as good, bad or in-between from the viewpoint of health, sanitation or water supply, etc. Common behaviours that can be made into picture cards for this exercise include washing hands with soap, sweeping trash into a pit, leaving food uncovered, painting the outside of a house, installing a rainwater catchment tank, swimming in a dirty pond, embroidering a table cloth.

NOTE TO TRAINER:

This activity further develops participants' self-confidence in analysing their own problems at the local level.

The adaptations of this exercise are limitless. At the trainer's level, it has been used as an evaluative tool to determine if trainees are able to differentiate among the different learning processes to which they have been exposed. For example, in one workshop, participants working in three groups were given strips of paper, each bearing the name of an activity done the previous day. The group's task was to sort out these activities into three categories: growth-oriented, message-focused, or in-be-

Samples of 3 Pile Sorting Cards

tween. Later the groups were invited to share their conclusions and defend them at a plenary session.

Participants were also urged to reconsider their classifications on the basis of the discussion and make changes if so indicated. They then realised that the trainer is not seeking absolute right answers but rather thoughtful analysis of all angles of the situation.

Extension staff can gain valuable insights from this activity into how people perceive their everyday behaviour in terms of its impact on health. In this sense, it becomes an investigative tool.

It can also serve as a preparation for planning, as when using it to sort out roles and responsibilities. For example, on a common problem of environmental sanitation, participants may identify a number of practical action steps and then ask: Who should take them? The community alone? The Government alone? Both?

PROCEDURES:

■ Form a circle.

■ Invite 2 or 3 volunteers to come to the centre of the circle. Give them the set of cards to study and then sort out into three piles: Good, Bad or In-Between, using good health, sanitation, water supply or other development conditions as criteria.

■ Encourage participants to reconsider their choices in consultation with other members of the group around them.

■ If some aspect has been missed, feel free to raise questions which would help the group think further and, if necessary, change their classification of the card concerned.

■ If desired, have participants select one or more cards from the Bad category and develop a list of action steps to resolve the problems presented. They should then decide who should be responsible for each step, i.e. the community, the government, or both jointly.

Here are some action steps that may be suggested:

■ Install pumps.

■ Build superstructures for latrines.

■ Take preventive measures against guinea worm.

■ Treat severe cases of infant malnutrition.

■ Start vegetable gardens using waste water.

■ Repair the pump.

■ Ensure that spare parts are available.

■ Monitor the proper use of water.

■ Pay for the costs of maintaining the water system.

■ Ensure the cleanliness of the community environment.

■ Ensure that women have a say in decisions.

This activity was introduced by Jacob Pfohl, Consultant.

Methods: Analytic

MINI-CASE STUDIES

PURPOSE:

To develop analytical skills.

TIME: 25-40 minutes

MATERIALS:

Copies of the case studies.

NOTE TO TRAINER:

This, like the "Critical Incident" Activity in this section on page 110, helps people to focus on their own problem-solving skills.

These are two mini-case studies that develop analytical skills.

PROCEDURES:

Village X Case Study

■ Ask participants to read the following hypothetical case study and make up data to fill in the blanks, based on their own experience.

■ Have them share their inputs with the rest of the group.

■ Ask them to prepare a group presentation of Mini-case Village X for discussion at a plenary session, particularly with regard to the *problem*.

CASE STUDY VILLAGE X

The Setting: In a small, remote and typical village called _____ with a population of _____ inhabitants, the illiteracy rate among men is _____% and among women _____%. The majority of women in the village must work _____ hours per day and have little opportunity to participate in community affairs. There is a high incidence of water-borne diseases such as _____.

The Problem: The government with the help of a highly skilled technical team introduced a water supply system two years ago at substantial cost. The system is no longer functioning. (Describe what is wrong with the system.)

The pump has fallen into disrepair due to _____

_____.

The technical team blames the people saying that they _____

_____.

The team also admits however that _____

_____.

The villagers feel _____

_____

Lubu Village Case Study

■ Ask the participants to study the case below and propose a plan of action in keeping with this centre's objective of instituting a community-based water and sanitation programme. Have them answer the following questions:

What additional information do you need?

What would be some key aspects of your plan of action?

LUBU VILLAGE CASE STUDY

The Lubu Community Centre is an indigenous organisation aiming to establish a community-based water and sanitation programme in Lubu Village. The Centre provides monetary and technical help to villagers.

In recent years, although the water supply and sanitation in the village have improved, there is still a series of problems to be faced. A meeting of the Lubu Committee has been called to discuss these problems.

The specific issues are as follows:

1. Even though water and latrines are provided, illnesses did not decrease.

2. Very few toilets are being used.

3. There is dependency on money and skills coming from outside the community.

4. The centre's funds are limited.

HEALTH CASE STUDY

PURPOSE:

To initiate discussion about community participation in local problems and how it can affect the outcome of projects.

TIME: 40-60 minutes

MATERIALS:

Newsprint or copies of the case study for each participant.

NOTE TO TRAINER:

This exercise gets participants talking about local situations and how they can improve their work with villagers.

The case study involves health and sanitation but it could be adapted for other sectors.

Participants can be provided copies of the entire case study and factors or you can read it aloud. They should be able to have a copy of the factors as they discuss the case.

The exercise can be done in a large group or three small groups.

PROCEDURES:

■ Read the following case study to the participants. If possible, have the factors posted on newsprint and reveal them only after the story is finished.

- Ask the group to discuss:

  What is your opinion? Which team is right?

  If you were an adviser to the project, what plan of action would you recommend to ensure effective usage and maintenance of water resources, as well as hygienic behaviours?

- Ask them how this learning applies to their own jobs and situations.

HEALTH CASE STUDY

The health engineering department of a local Government Ministry had launched a project to provide 60,000 villages with four tubewells each, over a 3-year period. In spite of organisational and logistical problems, by the end of its second year, the project was reaching two-thirds of the villages and was seen as a masterful job of management assistance. The people, however, were reluctant to contribute towards maintenance costs and many tubewells were showing signs of neglect or misuse.

In addition, a survey by a diarrhoeal research team showed that in many villages where wells were provided, diarrhoeal rates showed no decline. In fact, there was a sharp increase of diarrhoea in several villages where people supposedly had safe water.

The team attributed this to the fact that no real effort seemed to have been made to involve the people in decision-making and to raise their awareness of the health consequences of unhygienic practices. In particular the team noted that the following factors may have contributed to the deteriorating local situation:

- Feelings of helplessness, apathy or fatalism in regard to common ailments such as diarrhoea.
- Dependence on external resources to solve problems for the community.
- Belief that initiatives and responsibilities incurring costs (such as maintenance of improved water systems) are beyond the meagre financial resources of the community.
- Belief that those who installed the system should care for it and bear the costs.
- Belief that water, being God's gift, should not require payment.
- Lack of experience in group planning and in mobilising resources for problem-solving, particularly among women.
- Low value placed on women's contribution to community level decision-making.
- A long tradition of hierarchical relations by which only a few speak on behalf of the many at community meetings, and decision-making is generally left to prestigious leaders.
- Mistaken beliefs and obsolete local practices associated with the prevention and cure of illnesses, presenting serious obstacles to behavioural change.

The department of engineering rejected the study. They suggested that the real problem was insufficient numbers of wells. "You cannot expect people to keep clean if there is not enough water for everyone. If there had been eight tubewells, the rates of diarrhoea would be bound to go down."

The case study was contributed by Jacob Pfohl, Consultant.

OPEN-ENDED PROBLEM DRAMA

PURPOSE:

To introduce trainers to evocative, open-ended stories that can stimulate discussion among villagers.

TIME: 30-50 minutes

MATERIALS:

Two stories one of which is "closed", i.e. has a conclusion, and the other open-ended.
Maxi-flans.

NOTE TO TRAINER:

This exercise should help trainers learn how to design learning material that can stimulate discussion and serve as an investigative tool for extension workers.

You can create two stories from local situations, such as a problem that the person might face that was resolved and another one in which there is no clear resolution. In the latter, the drama is built around a central character who has a problem and is subject to conflicting advice on how to solve it from two or three other characters. The main character is thus faced with a dilemma: Whose opinion is correct? Whose advice should one follow?

PROCEDURES:

■ Divide the participants into small groups of four or five persons each.

■ Tell the groups you will present two stories, one of which is open-ended and the other "closed", i.e. it has a conclusion. They should listen to both stories and decide which one is open-ended and which is closed.

■ Get feedback from all groups and discuss until a consensus is reached.

■ When the open-ended story has been identified, ask the same groups to study it carefully and list its characteristics, including such items as length, number of characters, and the way in which the listeners become involved in the story. Ask them what made it a good or not-so-good example to learn about the participants.

■ As a group, ask them to develop guidelines for putting together an open-ended drama. These are some examples of the guidelines which can emerge from this discussion:

- Be brief.

- Be focused on a problem which is relevant to the audience.

- Have one main character affected by the problem.

- Include no more than three other characters.

- Have each one give contradictory advice.

- Present advice in a clear way that the audience can take sides.

- Leave the main character undecided on the right course of action.

- Ask the audience to suggest the conclusion.

■ Invite participants to write and share their own problem-drama episodes using illustrations. Working in three subgroups, participants can learn more about the technique through discussion, comparison and peer critique of the problem-drama. They could also role play the characters if they wish.

MAXI-FLANS

The SARAR material called maxi-flans can be used to liven up the story and to make the characters more memorable.

Like flexis, maxis are cut-out figures to be displayed on flannel board but they are large (approximately two feet [.6 m] high from the torso up) and they are limited to the three or four principal characters named in the problem-drama.

The main character is introduced first and placed in the centre of the flannel board. Then, as the story unfolds, each of the remaining characters is introduced one by one as they come to give the main character their opinion or advice.

Names given to each character may be written on cards and placed alongside the corresponding maxi. Even if some participants are illiterate, the name cards seem to help in identifying the different personalities during the discussion that follows, as audience members take sides with one character or another.

During such a discussion many private beliefs and feelings may be aired and many local undercurrents may surface. The facilitators must be prepared to handle all such data as privileged information.

Based on the problem-drama techniques used by World Education in Turkey.

CRITICAL INCIDENT

PURPOSE:

To help villagers develop analytical ability in order to solve local problems.

TIME: 20-30 minutes

MATERIALS:

Pictures or drawings of problem situations.

NOTE TO TRAINER:

As noted earlier, in development activities at the village level, analysis is needed to understand the dimensions of a problem, to identify the most logical and efficient procedures to arrive at solutions and to define the precise investment implications for manpower, funds or equipment. This is one of several analytical exercises for villagers. See also the "Mini-Cases" Activity in this section on page 104.

A Critical Incident activity is similar to the Problem-Drama in that it involves analysis of the pros and cons of proposed solutions. Structurally, it can be simpler and shorter, especially if a set of visuals is used to illustrate the circumstances leading up to the crisis.

For example, at a Training of Trainers workshop in Lesotho, one subgroup presented a critical incident in the life of a rural household that had no latrine. The story was developed with the help of three visuals: The first one showed an angry husband refusing to build a latrine; the second showed the wife going out to the bush on a rainy night due to lack of household sanitary facilities; the third showed the wife ill with fever, the house neglected and the husband looking very worried.

PROCEDURES:

■ Present two or three visuals that illustrate a problem situation.

■ Ask the group to analyse what problem is being conveyed in the pictures, what factors might have contributed to the problem and how it could be resolved.

■ Discuss the pros and cons of different options.

A VILLAGE WATER COMMITTEE

PURPOSE:

To introduce participants to the concept of cost/benefit analysis in the context of village water sources.

To have them go through a decision-making process similar to that required of a village water committee.

To have them compare the outcomes of their discussions with those of a real village water committee in Indonesia.

TIME: 45 minutes

MATERIALS:

A mini-case as follows:

> A small village some 30 km [19 miles] from Kupang had a hand-dug well, about 28 meters [92 ft.] deep. It cost Rp 10,000 and took the people three years to dig. The location of the well was chosen because of a big tree in the immediate area that stayed green during the dry season.

> The water source used before the well existed was a spring in a distant cave with a very steep climb down to the water.

> A Mark II handpump was put in by the government without organising the village beforehand. The pump worked for a few months and then broke. The village asked the government for help. The government replied that the pump belonged to the village now and asked them what they were going to do to keep it working. After many stops and starts, a Water Committee has now been formed.

> The Committee's first task is to consider the costs and benefits of repairing the pump, or removing it or reverting to the original spring source.

Its next task is to prepare a plan of action to ensure that its chosen water source will be kept in good order.

If you were a member of the Water Committee, what would you suggest be done?

PROCEDURES:

■ Have participants read the mini-case and discuss possible actions by the committee. After they have discussed it, share with them the following description of decisions taken by the Indonesian village committee to cover costs and ensure proper use and maintenance.

- Each family pays Rp 250 per month to collect drinking water. They pay an additional Rp 500 if they want to use the water for gardening, and another Rp 400 if they want water for cattle.

- Each family has an assigned time to collect its water; this prevents waiting lines at the well.

- Each family uses about 20 pails of water a day for drinking, cooking and washing.

- If water is used for gardening, then the family must plant at least five rows of crop: one row goes to PKK the sponsoring agency; another to the Water Committee; and the remaining rows to the family.

- Once a month a notice is posted on the palm tree near the well, reminding everyone to pay their monthly dues; if they don't pay, they cannot continue to collect water from the well.

- The village also has three subcommittees: one to collect dues; one to make sure people are not wasting water; and one for maintenance.

- Maintenance involves replacing the gaskets and chains; the pump has broken seven times in the last three years, but villagers can usually do the pump repairs themselves.

Adapted from an exercise developed by Fran Keally, Consultant.

WATER TRANSPORTATION AND STORAGE

PURPOSE:

To help participants analyse how water drawn from the pump can become contaminated before it is consumed in the home and what can be done to prevent this contamination (or what can be done to purify contaminated water).

TIME: 1 hour

MATERIALS:

Three pictures depicting:

1. Two women getting water at a pump

2. A man or a child drinking a glass of dirty water

3. Another man or child drinking a glass of clean water

PROCEDURES:

■   Participants examine the picture of women getting water at the pump and describe what is happening, what the names of the two women are and whether the water they have gotten from the pump is clean. The picture is then attached to the board.

■   Participants then study the picture of the person drinking the dirty water. Trainer explains that this is (one of the women's names) husband or child, on the next day, drinking the water she brought home from the pump. The picture is attached to the board at some distance from the pump picture with an arrow between the two:

Pump   →   Dirty Water
(Picture 1)   (Picture 2)

The trainer asks, "What could have happened between the first and second picture to cause the water to have become contaminated?"

When all the possible reasons (events) have been described, the trainer attaches the second picture (person drinking clean water) below the picture of the person drinking dirty water and explains that this is the husband/child of the second woman at the pump. An arrow is drawn between the pump picture and the clean water picture:

Pump   Dirty Water
(Picture 1)   (Picture 2)

                  → Clean Water
                    (Picture 3)

The trainer asks, "What has this woman done to keep her drinking water clean?"

Participants discuss what can be done in a village to help people keep their pump water clean.

Adapted from an exercise developed by Agma Prins, Consultant.

WATER COMMITTEE RESPONSIBILITIES

PURPOSE:

To help participants analyse the possible roles of the pump committee in the village.

TIME: 45 - 60 minutes

MATERIALS:

Assorted flexi-flan figures of men and women. Other flexi figures including children and a variety of "props" (houses, trees, animals, pump, etc.) to be used in creating a village scene. (See sample flexis in the activity on "Flexi-flans as Creative Materials" [*Methods/Creative*] on page 83).

PROCEDURES:

■ Have participants seated in three groups.

■ Invite each group to send two representatives to the table where the flexis are spread out. They are to choose one flexi each (male or female) to represent a village pump committee member.

■ Upon returning to their groups they should explain to their peers why they chose those particular figures to represent pump committee members: what qualities they seem to possess, what functions they seem capable of fulfilling, and why. The group should discuss and elaborate on these ideas and make a list of the functions they believe their committee members are capable of fulfilling.

■ The three groups should introduce their "committee members" in a plenary session; they are to post their lists of functions and comment on them verbally.

■ Next, the three lists of functions are to be compared, discussed and consolidated in the plenary. Additional ideas that arise from this discussion should be incorporated into the list.

■ Throughout the activity, the participants should freely contribute from their village level field experience to propose functions and assess their feasibility.

Adapted from an activity introduced by Agma Prins and Ron Sawyer.

STORY WITH A GAP

PURPOSE:

To demonstrate how villagers as a group can be engaged in planning water, sanitation and health activities.

To show how visuals can help to simplify the planning process.

TIME: 45-60 minutes

MATERIALS:

Two large posters, one of which shows a "before" scene (a problem situation) and the other an "after" scene (a greatly improved situation or solution to the problem).

A set of smaller pictures showing some of the steps which could be taken in moving from the problem to the solution.

NOTE TO TRAINER:

This planning exercise can be adapted by the trainers for village use.

The involvement of local communities requires a certain ability to plan. Average community members, and women in particular, may not have experience in such planning. This activity helps to simplify the planning process.

If appropriate pictures are not available, you can draw some with stick figures. You can also have the participants draw them. In the second step, participants can brainstorm the steps in between the "before" and "after" instead of using pictures.

Sometimes we include some seemingly irrelevant pictures in the set and give the groups the option of discarding any pictures they consider inappropriate. Usually they will attach some meaning, often humourous, to the less relevant pictures and incorporate them into their planning strategy. This added dimension of creativity increases the enjoyment of the exercise.

PROCEDURES:

■ Divide the participants into two or three subgroups.

■ Present the "before" picture to the participants and either invite their comments on what they see or personalise the scene by telling them about a family that lived in that village (give names, details of health hazards etc.) Build the story up to a crisis point where something had to be done to improve conditions.

■ Ask them to speculate on why the village situation has deteriorated. For example, if the picture includes a broken pump, participants may suggest the following: too many users, no caretakers, lack of maintenance knowledge, lack of spare parts, well is dry, children misuse it, vandalism, animals destroy the apron.

■ Having established the "before" baseline situation, introduce the "after" picture and allow time for the group to discuss it, noting the substantial improvements achieved.

■ Next raise the question: What steps do you think the village people took in changing the conditions of their village from "before" to "after"? Here, have the group brainstorm or, if necessary, distribute the pictures of steps. You could include blank cards among the pictures for participants to add steps of their own.

Before

After

119

Sample Story with a Gap "Steps"

CARTS AND ROCKS

PURPOSE:

To involve village participants in the analysis of **resources** and **constraints** related to the achievement of a set goal.

TIME: 30-45 minutes

MATERIALS:

Any locally available cheap materials or found objects that can be used to represent: a cart, rocks to put in the cart, and beasts to pull the cart.

PROCEDURES:

■ Engage participants in a discussion of a local problem they would like to resolve or situation they would like to improve, thus setting a goal to be achieved. Use an appropriate object to symbolise the goal.

■ Using a large found object such as an empty box to represent a cart, place it some distance from the goal but facing in the direction of the goal. The cart represents the community aspiring to move towards the goal. Then ask the group what resources are available to help them succeed in this effort. For each resource identified place an object in front of the cart symbolising an animal harnessed to pull the cart towards the goal.

■ Similarly, ask the group to identify the constraints to goal achievement. For each constraint identified, let the group place an object (e.g. a rock) in the cart suggesting additional weight to carry or forces holding people back. The size of the rock selected should correspond to the complexity or weight of the constraint it represents. Ask the group to assess the likelihood of the cart reaching its destination (overcoming the current problem).

■ Encourage the group to make realistic judgments so that the model can accurately reflect the real situation. The positive and negative forces should be analysed one by one, and in relation to each other, for example, by considering which resource could be most helpful in overcoming any given constraint.

Based on an activity introduced by Charles Harns, Consultant.

PUMP REPAIR ISSUES

PURPOSE:

To help participants analyse the factors influencing village pump repair and to plan initial strategies to deal with pump breakdown.

TIME: 45 - 60 minutes

MATERIALS:

Three pictures of:

- a water vendor with a broken down cart
- a broken pump, dirty environment and people arguing
- a clean working pump with people drawing water

A series of smaller pictures showing possible steps in pump repair, for example:

- a group meeting
- people giving money
- someone using tools to repair the pump
- people talking to an "official"
- someone with a pump part in his or her hand
- someone walking on the road
- people discussing around the pump
- people cleaning the pump area

(Some blank cards should be included. Ideally duplicate sets of these steps should be available, one for each group).

PROCEDURES:

■ Show the picture of the water vendor, Ahmed, (or pick an appropriate name), with the broken down cart. Invite the participants to suggest what Ahmed needs to do to have his cart repaired.

■ Show the next picture (of a broken pump) explaining that it belongs to village X (give the village a name). Ask the participants what the villagers must do to repair their pump. Compare it with what Ahmed does to repair his cart. Who is responsible in each case? Who pays? Which is more difficult to keep in good order? Why?

■ Have the groups report their conclusions in a plenary session. Next place the picture of the broken pump on the board and put a card marked NOW above it. Place the picture of the good pump some distance away on the same board and put a card marked ONE MONTH LATER above it.

■ Ask participants to return to their groups and study the "Now" and the "Later" pictures. They should discuss what could have happened in between to improve the "Now" situation. What steps could the village have taken? What did they do first? and next? and so on.

■ Give each group a set of the smaller pictures representing steps; if copies are unavailable have them draw their own.

■ When ready ask the groups to display and compare their sequence of steps in a plenary session.

Adapted from a PROWWESS-assisted workshop in Kenya.

IMPERTINENT PERT CHART

PURPOSE:

To demonstrate a systematic way of planning an activity as a sequence of steps to be achieved within a set time-frame and with co-ordinated action along two or more fronts.

TIME: 1 1/2 to 2 hours

MATERIALS:

Newsprint or other large sheet of paper; markers, pencils, tape.

NOTE TO TRAINER:

A PERT (Programme Evaluation and Review Technique) Chart provides a system or framework for planning an action. It tells when an action should be started, by whom and for whom, what steps are required, in what sequences, what outputs are expected and what alternative decisions may be taken. The Impertinent Pert Chart (IPC) is an informal and simplified way of doing the same type of planning.

PROCEDURES:

■   Have participants select a problem to be addressed, for instance, unhygienic local practices.

■   Divide them into groups.

■   Ask them to raise questions, in their groups, to explore the full implications of the problem, for example: What is the nature of the problem? Who is affected? What are some ways to resolve it? What constraints stand in the way? What resources are available?

■ They should then:

   ■ select a specific objective related to the problem, to be achieved within a set time-frame, e.g. develop a kit of participatory health education materials for use by village volunteers, in particular women, to stimulate the adoption of hygienic behaviours. Time frame for production: 6 months.

   ■ brainstorm a number of action steps required to achieve that objective (the action ideas generated will be in no particular order).

   ■ evaluate the ideas generated and select those that are most pertinent and feasible.

   ■ write each action idea selected on a separate 2 X 3 inches [5 cm x 8 cm] card or slip of paper.

   ■ decide on three or four categories under which the action steps can be grouped, e.g. "Research", "Drafting", "Field Testing".

   ■ Use these categories as headings in preparing the left-hand side of the IPC.

■ To prepare the IPC the groups should:

   ■ Take a large sheet of paper and divide it horizontally into as many spaces as the number of categories identified. Write the category headings on the left-hand side. Leave a blank space above "Steps" for inserting specific blocs of time for the sequence of steps.

   ■ For each category, review the steps and stick them in the right-hand columns in a logical sequence beginning with that which is the easiest and/or most urgent step to take. Rearrange as necessary after discussion. Add any new steps needed.

   ■ Carefully review each step in terms of how much time it is likely to take and what costs, if any, will be involved. Note the time needed in the top left-hand corner of the action-step card. Note the cost, if any, in the top right-hand corner (or attach mini-sized play money).

   ■ Look at the time-frame slot at the top of the chart. Divide it into segments of months corresponding to the total time available for completing the activities.

■ Without disturbing the sequence of the steps corresponding to each category, the groups should:

   ■ Consider which steps of any one category would have to be undertaken before, after, or simultaneously with other steps of the other categories.

   ■ Space them accordingly to show how action will proceed along several fronts in a co-ordinated manner.

   ■ Divide the top horizontal space on the chart into time segments (e.g. months) adding up to the total time available for the activities. Then arrange the activities which have been previously sequenced above so that they are realistically spaced and stay within the total time available.

Adapted from the author's Impertinent PERT Chart published by World Education.

SARAR SANITATION HEALTH GAME

PURPOSE:

To demonstrate how a board game can combine information with decision-making by the players so that information becomes more meaningful to them.

To help trainees understand the uses and limitations of games as learning tools.

TIME: 1 hour

MATERIALS:

A sanitation/health board with a row of clean houses on the left and unsanitary houses on the right.

Six to twelve different tokens (or pebbles) representing "community members" to be placed in the unsanitary houses.

One token or rock of a different colour, shape and size to represent "Disease". It should be placed on any negative square in the centre of the board.

One die (or numbers one to six on slips of paper).

PROCEDURES:

■ Explain the game. Lay out the tokens on the board.

■ Have the participants decide who will play the role of "Community Members" (as one team) and of "Disease" as opponent.

■ Demonstrate how to play the game so that all the rules are understood.

RULES OF THE GAME:

"Community Members" must leave their unsanitary houses and reach the clean houses without getting caught by "Disease" along the way.

They can only travel in the direction of the arrow.

Once any "Community Member" enters a clean house he or she becomes a "Health Worker" and can come out to fight "Disease".

"Health Workers" can travel in either direction. So can "Disease".

Tokens can be moved only as many spaces as the number shown by the die when it is cast.

The "Community Member" players and the "Disease" player take turns at casting the die (i.e. "Disease" gets a turn after each "Community Member" has had a turn).

Any one "Community" team player after casting the die, can move any of the team's tokens so as to avoid landing in a negative square.

"Disease" can "knock off" a "Community" token from the game if it is in a negative space and if "Disease" throws the right number on the die as needed to reach that space while the "Community Member" is there.

A "Health Worker" can "knock off" "Disease" if the latter is in a positive space and if the "Health Worker" throws the right number on the die to reach that space while "Disease" is there.

The game ends when "Disease" has been removed from the board or when all "Community Members" and "Health Workers" have been "knocked out".

Based on a game developed by the author for a Save The Children workshop in the Dominican Republic.

JUEGO DE LA SALUD

DEVELOPING A MURAL ON COMMUNITY PARTICIPATION

PURPOSE:

To stimulate individual and group ideas on the meaning and forms of community participation, assist participants to reconcile diverse viewpoints and reach agreements.

TIME: 45-60 minutes

MATERIALS:

Paper, pencils, marking pens, coloured pencils.

NOTE TO TRAINER:

This exercise is especially helpful in illustrating different views of community participation among a very diverse group of trainees. The mural provides a vehicle for discussion leading to development of a common approach. The trainers can use this later with extension workers.

The participants are asked to use drawings rather than words for expressing their viewpoints, in order to increase the creative tension of the exercise.

Some participants may protest that they cannot draw. Urge them to use stick figures or symbols. Impress on them the value of using a new medium of communication which is creative and enjoyable.

PROCEDURES:

■   Divide the participants into three small groups of no more than ten members each.

■ Explain that this activity is to help the whole group understand how each member feels about community participation.

■ Ask participants to draw a picture illustrating their concept of community participation. They have 10 minutes in which to complete the task.

■ Ask each small group to share their individual drawings and to combine them into one display. Choose a spokesperson who can explain the display to the large group.

■ Have each small group present their concepts of community participation to the other participants.

■ With the help of an artist if available, all the drawings can be combined into a group mural of community participation for use at the closing ceremony.

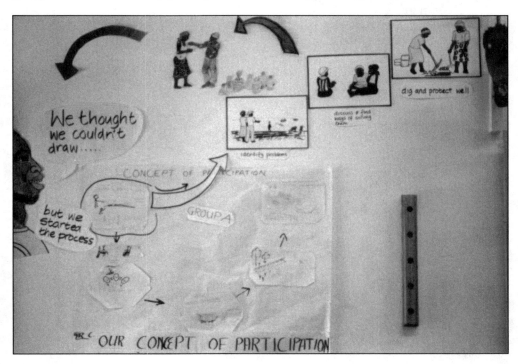

WOMEN'S PARTICIPATION IN WSS

PURPOSE:

Sensitisation to women's role in the Water Supply and Sanitation sector.

TIME: 30-40 minutes

MATERIALS:

Copies of the article "Whose Project?", and the discussion questions for participants to study, preferably one to two persons per copy.

NOTE TO TRAINER:

This activity can be used with any group of trainees but is particularly useful for sensitising hardware-oriented personnel. If you can try it simultaneously with both "hardware" and community level workers with "software" experience, i.e. those who have worked intimately with village people in participatory ways, the contrast will provide for a rich learning exchange.

PROCEDURES:

- ■ Divide the group into subgroups of not more than 5-6 persons each.
- ■ Distribute the article and discussion questions.
- ■ Ask participants to note down ideas individually or in pairs before discussing with other members of their subgroup.
- ■ Have participants share the conclusions of their subgroup in a plenary session.

Whose Project?

All the way in our jeep the programme officer elaborated clearly and convincingly that "the project must belong to the community, it must be their project, not the agency's project, not the government's project, but the community's own project". He, the *lurah* (the Indonesian village head man), and I stood inspecting the water hand-pump and its apron. We faced each other in a close knot while children, women, and a few men assembled and stood respectfully some way off looking at our backs. Three or four little girls were hunched down under the mouth of the pump, washing clothes by pounding them with sticks. Anyone coming for water would have to push them aside (as did one woman who placed her baby's soiled bottom under the spout).

I asked our community-oriented officer whether it would be good practice to separate the laundry and ablutions from under the pump which had been installed primarily to supply clean drinking water. "Yes of course." How would one design a place for doing the washing in this village? Would the villagers prefer to squat, stand, sit at a central trough and talk to each other? He replied "I don't really know, I'll ask the *lurah*". I suggested instead we ask the large audience of ladies who were standing and staring at we *orang tinggi* (high persons). When the programme officer humoured me and put the question to them, they all began to laugh. "They are laughing", he said, "because they think it very strange; no one has ever asked them such things before!" So it seems no one had ever asked them how their project ought to be. How then could it really be their project?

Between the general theory of participation (or at least the rhetoric) and what actually happens in practice, a gap yawns.

By David Drucker, "Community Participation: Now you see it, now you don't," UNICEF News Issue 124/1986.

DISCUSSION QUESTIONS

1. What type of concept of participation is the author advocating?

2. Have you come across this kind of situation in your experience?

3. What are some reasons, in your opinion, for the limited involvement of women in conventional WSS projects (or in a specific setting known to you)?

4. If you were the community officer being interviewed by the author, what reasons would you give for not asking for women's opinions? List at least three reasons.

5. How would you evaluate whether the community is genuinely involved in the project of which you are the manager? What indicators would you use?

TWO CIRCLES EXERCISE

PURPOSE:

To analyse the needs and potential of women in relation to the water supply, sanitation and health situation of their community.

TIME: 45-60 minutes

MATERIALS:

Newsprint and markers. Village maps if developed by the group in an earlier activity. See the "Map building" Activity (*Methods/Investigative*), on page 99.

NOTE TO TRAINER:

This exercise is designed to generate ideas about increasing women's access to services and their role in planning and management decisions.

PROCEDURES:

■ Divide the participants into three small groups of no more than ten members each.

■ Give each small group newsprint and markers. (If they have done a map, ask them to use it as a reference point).

■ Have participants draw two circles on their newsprint: one large circle enclosing a smaller circle. The larger circle is to represent the village context; the smaller circle is to depict women's situation.

■ Ask participants to write down in the larger circle all of the water, sanitation, and health-related problems that affect the community as a whole. In the inner circle they should note those problems which affect women in particular.

■ Upon completing these steps, participants should discuss in the large group:

How do the problems in the two circles differ?

How are they complementary?

What solutions can be found for both, with adequate priority given to women's needs?

What action can you take, upon returning to your own agency, to help address women's problems and enhance their roles in community participation?

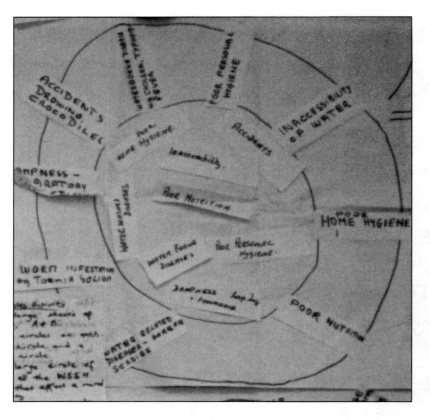

BALLOON EXERCISE

PURPOSE:

To involve participants in an analysis of women's situation in terms of the chain of consequences that result from any one problem faced by them.

TIME: 45-60 minutes

MATERIALS:

Newsprint and markers.

PROCEDURES:

■ Divide participants into small groups of no more than ten members each.

■ Give each group a set of markers and newsprint.

■ Ask them to begin by drawing or pasting a picture of a village woman in the lower left-hand corner. Close to this picture they should draw a balloon in which they should note down one major problem affecting women.

■ They should then reflect on one or more consequences resulting from the first problem. For each consequence, they should draw a new balloon and link it to the first, indicating that it is a consequence of the first problem. They should continue drawing and linking other balloons representing the consequence of those consequences.

■ When a whole chain of balloons has been created in this way they should reflect on *how* and *where* the chain of negative consequences can be broken.

■ The small groups should sum up their thinking on women's situation based on this exercise and share it in a plenary session.

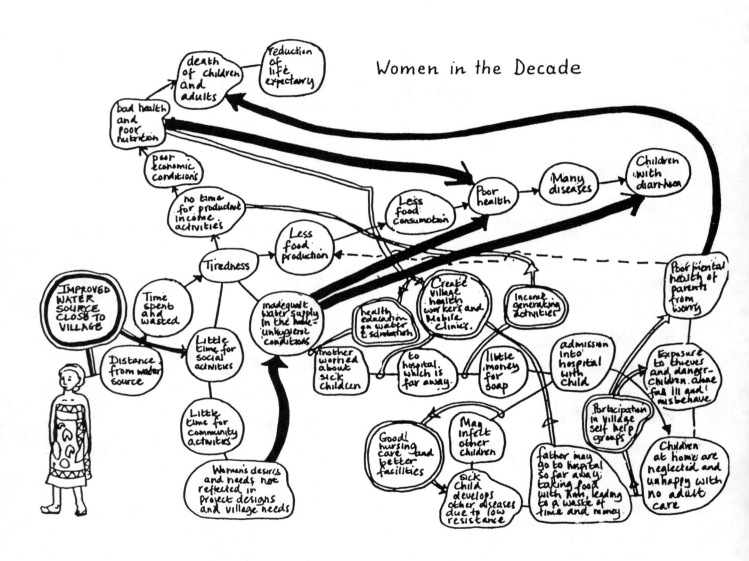

Women in the Decade

Double-lined circles are solutions

Single-lined circles are problems

From a PROWWESS workshop in Tanzania

A WEEK IN THE LIFE OF A VILLAGE HEALTH WORKER (VHW)

PURPOSE:

To reach a common understanding of the realities of a village health worker's work-load so that the expectations of supervisory and technical personnel do not exceed the VHW's capacity to deliver services.

To assess the amount of time spent by VHWs in community education activities and what kind of support they need to fulfil this function.

TIME: Under 1 hour

MATERIALS:

Newsprint, markers, paper, glue.

NOTE TO TRAINER:

This exercise provides an essential glimpse into the reality of the work of extension workers. There is a tendency to expect the extension worker to perform miracles in mobilizing community participation. There is also a tendency to minimise or simply brush aside the numerous and tedious demands made on the extension worker's time and energy by supervisory staff. Those who train, supervise and rely on extension staff need to understand that reality.

This exercise was first tried in a workshop in Zimbabwe where the composition of the subgroups was multi-level. They included different categories of staff such as health inspectors, health educators, public health nurses and health assistants. Through their combined experience and through probing from different angles, each subgroup came up with their own perception of how a village health worker functions over a week-long period. (See the list on page 141.) In the process of producing, comparing and evaluating these scenarios, many important insights were gained and a more realistic perspective achieved.

PROCEDURES:

■ Divide the group into three small groups, each of which has representation from the various functional levels of the health delivery system.

■ Ask the groups to pool their knowledge as to what tasks a VHW performs during one week. Each activity is to be written on a small square piece of paper and taped to the calendar.

■ The three groups consolidate their week's activity list into one master calendar which might include activities like those on the following sample list from the workshop in Zimbabwe.

■ Ask the participants to circle or check all of the activities that are potentially educational opportunities for community groups or individuals. Only those activities which require the use of educational strategies should be highlighted in this way.

■ They should also mark those activities on the VHW's calendar which are likely to meet with the greatest resistance or skepticism.

■ Ask participants to summarise what they have learned from this exercise.

Note: *If you want to link this activity with the "Resistance to Change Continuum" and "Johari's Window" Activities (Theory), have participants select any one activity from the calendar which lends itself most to the use of educational strategies. Ask the group what kinds of beliefs, customs, traditions, attitudinal and practical obstacles the VHW might encounter in trying to implement the activity and what educational techniques and/or materials would be needed for this purpose. In this way participants will be reminded to look for the essential link between their own roles, those of the VHW and participatory educational methods.*

A Week In the Life of a Village Health Worker

Talk to supervisor reorganising for building latrines.	Check how many wells in the village need protecting.	Prepare a report on the number of new water points in the village.
Arrange for building of demonstration latrines.	Report on the number of toilets that have been built.	Make sure that mothers are present for the immunisation programme. Encourage them to stay.
Be present for inspection of beer halls.	Select a village for a donor's visit.	Treat minor ailments.
Do house-to-house visits.	Find out people's complaints and pass them on to the District office.	Keep a diary of weekly activities.
Identify felt needs of the people.	Find out if people are interested in raising rabbits.	Motivate people to build toilets.
Organise a village meeting.	Identify malnourished children and report to the health clinic.	Check cases of TB, Malaria and Diarrhoea.
Attend village committee meeting when discussing health matters.	Inform people that cement has arrived; tell them "no digging toilets, no cement".	

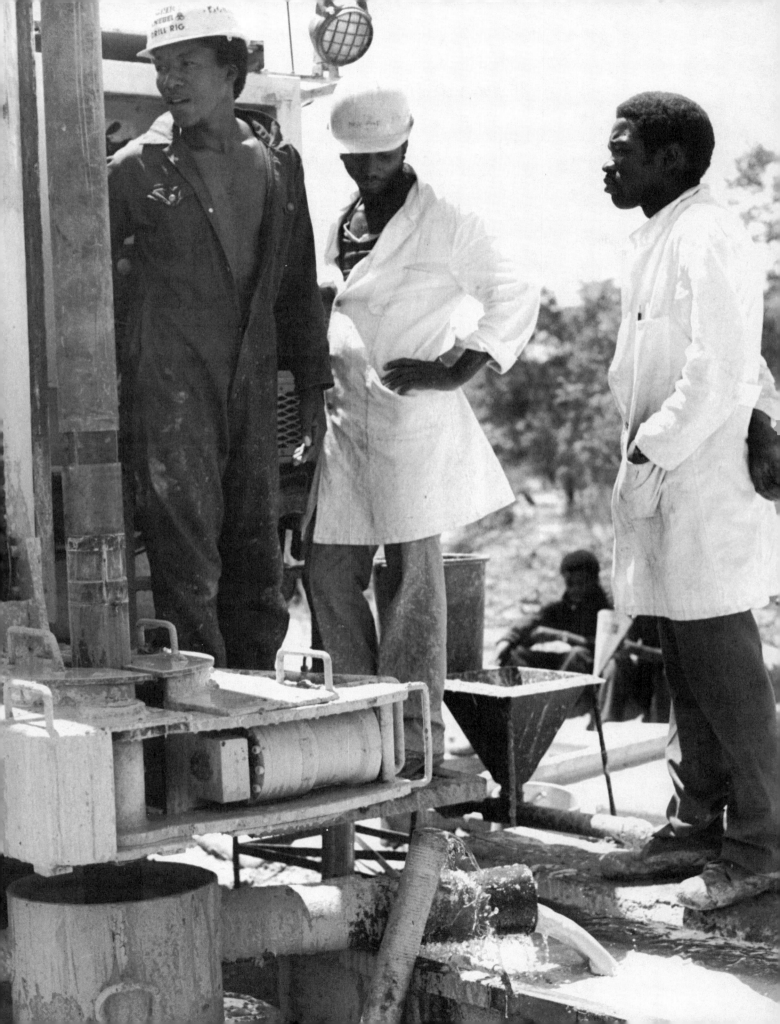

INTEGRATION OF HARDWARE AND SOFTWARE COMPONENTS

PURPOSE:

To make participants aware of the value of accommodating software concerns in hardware plans and vice versa, so as to reconcile the need to promote people's participation with the need to meet hardware deadlines.

TIME: 1 1/2 -2 hours

MATERIALS:

Typed list of hardware and software components with instructions (two or more copies per group). Also a copy of the hardware components alone on one large sheet of newsprint and the software components on another. Cut both the typed lists and the newsprint horizontally, starting from the right so as to separate each of the items, but leave a margin on the left so all the items are still connected. You then have a list from which individual strips can be easily detached and regrouped in a new sequence.

Newsprint, scissors, markers, masking tape.

NOTE TO TRAINER:

The exercise is a tough, challenging and absorbing assignment as the groups work together in developing an integrated plan. But, much mutual understanding can be developed about each group's distinctive needs and the complementary aspects of those needs.

PROCEDURES:

■ Divide the participants into four groups, of which two are composed of people knowledgeable about "hardware" and the other two about "software".

■ Distribute the typed lists to the four groups and allow time for them to read the instructions.

■ Explain that the two hardware groups should cut apart only the typed hardware list and the software group only the software list.

■ Ask them to rearrange the items cut apart in logical order, showing the sequence in which each step would be undertaken in an actual village setting.

■ Have the two hardware groups meet and reconcile their sequence of steps to produce one hardware sequence. Software groups should do the same.

■ Ask the groups to paste the larger newsprint strips of hardware and software components on the wall in the same order in which they arranged their cut-up typed strips. (If groups were not able to reconcile the steps, they can put up two examples instead of one.)

■ Each of the sections (hardware and software) should form a team to decide at which points the hardware/software sequences could best be integrated.

■ Facilitate a plenary discussion in which all lists are compared and integrated as much as possible.

■ Ask participants to identify items which they believe would be appropriate for planning jointly with community members; as well as those which are considered to be the primary responsibility of the community alone or the agency alone. This should give rise to much heated discussion and result in useful insights for policy and management.

Hardware

Arrange for supply of spare parts

Conduct geological survey

Hold planning meetings

Select a village

Brief the hydrologist

Plan use of area around pump

Establish drilling

Compile village files

Purchase drills, vehicles, and other supplies

Ensure delivery of pumps

Do aerial photo study of the area

Conduct pump trials

Plan drilling campaigns

Map the selected village

Select site for a pump

Software

Create a village fund

Promote women's participation

Evaluate use of water source

Hold community meetings about the project

Discuss agency and community roles in the project

Select site for a pump

Evaluate project impact

Meet with local leaders

Train trainers

Register the Water Committee

Help community open a bank account

Make informal contacts between project staff and community members

Sign land agreement for placing the pump

Conduct participatory needs assessment

Form water committees

Collect money within the community

Plan training activities

Conduct learner-centred educational activities

Select and train new water source caretakers

Train village committee members

Conduct hygiene education

ROLE PERCEPTIONS

PURPOSE:

To understand and clarify perceptions about people's roles in different sectors and at different levels.

TIME: 1 hour

MATERIALS:

Newsprint.

NOTE TO TRAINER:

This exercise helps to overcome misconceptions or unrealistic expectations that staff within a ministry or other organisation may have of one another.

On occasion you may find yourself called upon to train a group that is multi-level within one ministry. To have such a diverse group interact can be a very rich experience. In the process, you may find that they know very little about each other's day-to-day functions. Without role clarity, team work even within one agency becomes difficult.

With this problem in mind, this exercise was developed to help participants "see themselves as others see them" and to create genuine willingness to compare and discuss mutual role expectations.

PROWWESS attempted this in one workshop by dividing participants into subgroups according to their specialties and professional categories. Each subgroup then proceeded to define roles for three distinct levels including their own. The activity turned out to be a highly charged one. The heated discussion that followed led to some serious thought as to what can be expected realistically of each level of the delivery system. The insights gained in this way seemed to help participants to be better prepared for follow-up planning by teams.

Supportive multi-sectoral relationships can also be built through the joint training of personnel from different extension services. PROWWESS did this in Lesotho among representatives of district rural sanitation programmes and a cross-section of village health workers. In this situation, we formed intersectoral, rather than specialty, teams and each team was responsible for planning, executing and evaluating village-based activities. In this way, they developed a stronger commitment to collaborative efforts in achieving the rural sanitation objectives of the programme.

PROCEDURES:

■   Divide the group into subgroups according to their professional specialty or level.

■   Ask each subgroup to define their own role and the roles of one group immediately below and one group immediately above their own. Members should write out the roles as they perceive them.

■   Have all the groups post the results in horizontal rows, one under the other, in such a way that the roles of any one category as seen from different perspectives can be compared in a vertical direction. Participants can walk around and observe the perceptions of all the other groups.

■   Discuss in the large group the discrepancies in views about each role and the implications for future team planning. Ask them for suggestions of how to work together more effectively now that they understand each other's roles better.

Theory

ATTRIBUTES FOR GOOD COMMUNITY PARTICIPATION

PURPOSE:

To help participants visualise the implication of "community participation" in terms of attitudes, dispositions, behaviours, capabilities, etc. which village people may need to have and utilise in order to become fully effective as partners in development.

TIME: 45-60 minutes

MATERIALS:

Qualities and Abilities List: Some Possible Attributes
Envelopes containing cut-up list pieces.

PROCEDURES:

■   Explain to the participants that in this activity there is no right or wrong answer but that they will each have to justify the choices they make. In so doing, they should draw from their own personal experience or knowledge of working with village people.

■   Hand out an envelope to each participant. Explain that each envelope has 32 slips of paper, of which 29 have words depicting certain attitudes, dispositions, behaviours,and capabilities. Many of these attributes (but not all) are what one might hope to find in village people when they are ready to "participate" in WSS program-mes. Some may not apply at all. The blank slips are in case participants wish to add to the list.

■   Ask the participants to carefully review all 29 attributes and choose five which in their personal opinion are the most vital to a programme which depends on full, effective and responsible participation by the people. (Do not exceed five; tightness of choice is important. Participants will have to think harder and draw more deeply from their experience in defense of their choices. Also it is important to stick to the same number for all. To give participants leeway to choose "between 3 and 5" for example, will give uneven results).

■ Divide participants into small subgroups — around five or six per group. The five attributes should be chosen first by each group member independently and then discussed and consolidated into one list for the group. They should prepare a written report explaining the group's reasons behind each choice. Allow 15 to 20 minutes.

■ Invite participants to share their reports in a plenary session. If time permits, have them consolidate all lists into one.

■ Suggest that participants reflect on the implications of their list of choices. To promote those qualities and attributes at the community level, what kind of educational strategy would be most appropriate?

■ Accept all suggestions and have one participant list them. These ideas will be reviewed later when alternative strategies are discussed.

Some Possible Attributes

Sense of Responsibility	Capacity to Make Rational Decisions	Resourcefulness
Capability to Generate New Ideas	Skill in Planning	Ability to Work Well in a Group
Initiative	Confidence in Articulating Ideas	Confidence in Relating to Authority Figures
Willingness to Take Risks	Willingness to Pay for Basic Services	Ability to Sort Out Priorities
Technical Know-How	Skill in Maintenance of Hardware	Leadership
Political Connections	Willingness to Accept Advice without Questioning	Willingness to Deviate from Community Values, Beliefs, and Customs
Sense of Humour	Savings Habit	Land Ownership
Humility	Willingness to Provide Free Labour or Materials	Acceptance of Women's Roles in Community Decision-Making
Ability to Participate in Constructive Group Discussions	Skill in Problem-Solving	Managerial Skills
Ability to Work Well on Committees	Enthusiasm	

This activity was specifically designed for a PROWWESS workshop in Burkina Faso.

Theory

PRINCIPLES OF ADULT LEARNING

PURPOSE:

To enable participants to reach an understanding of the principles upon which participatory training is based and which can be applied to training at the village level.

To help participants differentiate between a didactic and participatory approach to teaching.

TIME: 30 minutes

MATERIALS:

Newsprint.

NOTE TO TRAINER:

As a trainer, you will want to be sure that the participants' understanding of the principles of adult learning is deepened gradually over the entire training process. No single activity does it all. But there are at least three ways in which we can ensure that the growth of this understanding is cumulative:

- Through activities especially designed to engage participants in reflecting on adult learning.

- Through comparative analysis of the role of the facilitator and of the participants in a learning experience.

- Through comparative analysis of learner behaviours from one activity to another.

PROCEDURES:

■ Ask participants to open the book of their lives and select the best learning experiences they can recall.

■ Have participants pair off and describe the experiences in full to each other. Ask them to think about what made the experiences so good.

■ Have the large group share these reasons and list them on a flip chart.

■ Compare how adults learn with how children learn. Consider to what extent the following apply to participants' own experiences:

RESPECT. EXPERIENCE. IMMEDIACY. ACTION (learning by doing).

■ From these experiences and discussion, list on the flip chart the main points that should be observed if good learning is to take place among a group of adult learners.

This exercise was introduced by Jane Vella, Consultant.

Theory

PHOTO PARADE

PURPOSE:

To get to know participants' own perceptions of what is a "good" style of training when working with village people.

To help participants learn to distinguish between didactic and learner-centred communication styles and to identify the basic requirements for effective adult learning.

TIME: 1 hour

MATERIALS:

Three copies of a set of photographs (around 10 photos), representing a wide range of communication situations, ranging from highly directive to highly participatory. For example:

- A demonstration where learners are active.
- A demonstration where they are passive.
- A lecture to a large audience.
- A small group discussion.
- A hands-on group activity.
- A written task in a formal classroom setting.
- An informal exchange of views in a village setting.
- An out-patient clinic where the nurse is instructing mothers.
- A situation where the extension worker is the listener and village women are speaking in a lively fashion.
- A community project involving supervised physical labour by villagers.

Sample Photos for Photo Parade

NOTE TO TRAINER:

This activity helps participants learn about factors most or least conducive to good learning. Through their own experience, they learn to apply these conclusions to their work with community members.

The success of this exercise depends on the right choice of photos, the willingness of the facilitator to refrain from "teaching," and strict limitation of the number of photos selected as positive and negative by each group. Any more than two of each category can make the reporting tedious. It is also important that the number of choices should be the same for all three groups.

This exercise is similar to the "Unserialised Posters" Activity (*Methods/Creative*), page 89. However, that activity emphasised imagination, whereas "Photo Parade" encourages logic and good judgement.

PROCEDURES:

■ Divide the participants into three groups and give each group an identical set of photographs.

■ Explain the task: "In your group, please look closely at your set of photographs and select the two photos you like the best and two which you like the least. Your choice should be based on the quality of the learning or communication that seems to be taking place in each case. Be prepared to report in 15 minutes and justify your choices. You should also write down your comments on each picture you have chosen, so that your ideas can be included in the workshop report."

■ Do not give the groups any clarification of the content of the photographs; they should be free to interpret them as they see fit.

■ When the task is completed, invite each group in turn to post the four photographs they have chosen on the blackboard, placing the two negative photos side by side on the left and the two positive ones on the right. The next groups will place their photos directly below, in the same order.

■ Each group must give its reasons for categorising their choices as positive or negative.

Adapted from an activity designed by Chris Srinivasan for a workshop in the Philippines.

CUP EXERCISE

PURPOSE:

To help participants clearly see the difference between directive and non-directive approaches as well as become aware of the fine gradations of directiveness/non-directiveness in a set of tasks.

To introduce a tool which can serve as a yardstick for measuring the degree of control or freedom implicit in a variety of learning tasks.

This exercise provides a tool to understand the role of the trainer in adult learning and how the highly directive or highly open trainer can influence the behaviour of participants.

TIME: 15-20 minutes

MATERIALS:

Sets of seven cards, each of which has a picture of a cup but with different instructions to go with it in mixed up order, for example:

- Put some coffee in the cup.
- Fill the cup to the brim with hot coffee.
- Do what you like with the cup.
- Put some liquid in the cup.
- Fill the cup with hot coffee.
- Put something in the cup.

There should be enough sets of cards for participants to work in pairs or in small groups of three to four persons.

PROCEDURES:

■ Invite the participants to arrange the cards in an order which indicates differences in degrees of directiveness or control starting with the most directive card on the left and ending with the most open on the right. The chances are that with minimal effort they will all get it right.

■ You may wish to ask them why it is that they all came up with the same answer. (The material was designed in such a way that there could only be one "right" answer.)

■ Encourage the group to comment on how the exercise can help them to understand the difference between didactic teaching materials and open-ended learning materials.

■ Invite them to consider at which points of this continuum they would place the workshop activities done that day, or the previous day.

The Cup Exercise

Put something in the cup

?

Fill the cup to the brim with hot coffee

Put some liquid in the cup

Do what you like with the cup

Fill the cup with hot coffee

Fill the cup with some liquid

THREE SQUARES ASSESSMENT

PURPOSE:

To analyse workshop experiences in terms of the degree of dominance of the trainer compared to autonomous participation by the trainees.

TIME: 15-20 minutes

MATERIALS:

Three squares shaded or coded to indicate three different ratios of trainer/trainee dominance. The first square has a large shaded area indicating approximately ninety percent trainer dominance, the second is coded to 50/50 participation; and the third only ten percent trainer dominance.

NOTE TO TRAINER:

This exercise helps clarify the concept of directive vs. non-directive educational strategies. It also helps participants realise that, although a trainer must work hard to prepare a learning exercise, if the task has been well-prepared, the trainer's role is simply to introduce it and let go; the task itself provides the structure within which the participants can operate on their own.

However, the amount of freedom which participants are able to exercise in responding will vary depending upon how much subject matter or content is already built into the materials utilised. It is extremely important for the extension workers to understand this principle.

Be prepared to list at least three activities from the programme that illustrate a range of trainer/participant control. Choose at least one in which their role was minimal, e.g. the "Cup Exercise" (*Theory*), and one where they have participated very actively, e.g. "Map Building" (*Methods/Investigative*).

PROCEDURES:

■ Remind participants of three or more activities in which they have recently participated. Do not disclose your reasons for choosing those activities.

■ Show the Three Squares and explain that the shaded area of the square represents the facilitator's role and the light area stands for the participants' role.

■ Ask the participants which of the three squares represent how they acted during each of the activities you have selected for discussion.

■ Let the participants discuss freely among themselves. Avoid giving the "right answer". The answer must emerge from their own analysis and from mutual challenging. You can help by occasionally pointing to issues that have been overlooked and if necessary underscoring the difference between the structure (format) of a task and the content which it evokes, i.e. the difference between setting a task and fulfilling it.

Trainer/Trainees Participation Percentages

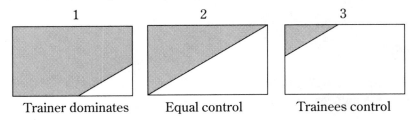

158

SOME POSSIBLE LEARNER BEHAVIOURS

PURPOSE:

To analyse behaviours that might result from didactic or participatory training activities.

TIME: 20-30 minutes

MATERIALS:

List of behaviours on cards or a large chart.

NOTE TO TRAINER:

This exercise helps people to think about certain behaviours that result from different types of training and prepares them to select appropriate training activities for the behavioural results they seek.

PROCEDURES:

■   Give participants the jumbled list of behaviours and ask them to sort the behaviours into two categories:

1.   Those you would expect in response to a didactic teaching lesson, such as a lecture.

2.   Those which might result from a participatory learner-centred activity.

■   Ask people to reflect on the two sets and to discuss which types of attitudes and attributes are helpful if people are to play a partnership role in development.

SOME POSSIBLE LEARNER BEHAVIOURS

Learners remember the content presented to them.

Learners organise themselves for planning and implementing solutions to problems relevant to their daily lives.

Learners initiate questions and challenge each other until concepts are clarified.

Learners answer questions posed by the instructor.

Learners engage in problem-solving on their own initiative.

Learners engage in a learning task with minimal promoting or support from a resource person.

Learners give the "correct answer" as taught by the instructor.

Learners contribute life experiences and ideas to group discussions.

Learners experience a high level of energy release and enthusiasm.

Learners suggest problems or topics on which they would like more information.

Learners are able to demonstrate in practice what they have learnt.

Learners become highly creative and inventive.

SARAR RESISTANCE TO CHANGE CONTINUUM (RTCC)

PURPOSE:

To sensitise participants to the fact that community members may have many different, often understandable reasons for not wishing to adopt change.

To demonstrate a simple way of categorising the resistances commonly met in the community so that differences in degree and types of resistances become clear.

To infer from this analysis which approaches would be most appropriate when working with people who are either receptive or resistant to change.

TIME: 1 hour - 1 1/2 hours

MATERIALS:

A blackboard or large newsprint on which a continuum diagram is drawn, showing seven stages of resistance or openness to change. (Sometimes eight stages may be identified, adding one more to the positive end of the continuum).

A variety of flexi-flans or other cut-out pictures of village people.

Balloon-shaped cut-outs, each of which has a quotation written on it representing the feeling or attitude of individual villagers towards a proposed change. There should be enough of these balloon quotes to correspond to all the stages of the continuum, with duplicates and some blanks.

A poster with a message to which there generally is some resistance in village communities, such as "Boil or filter river water before drinking" or "Use latrines and not the 'bush' for defecation."

SARAR Resistance To Change Continuum

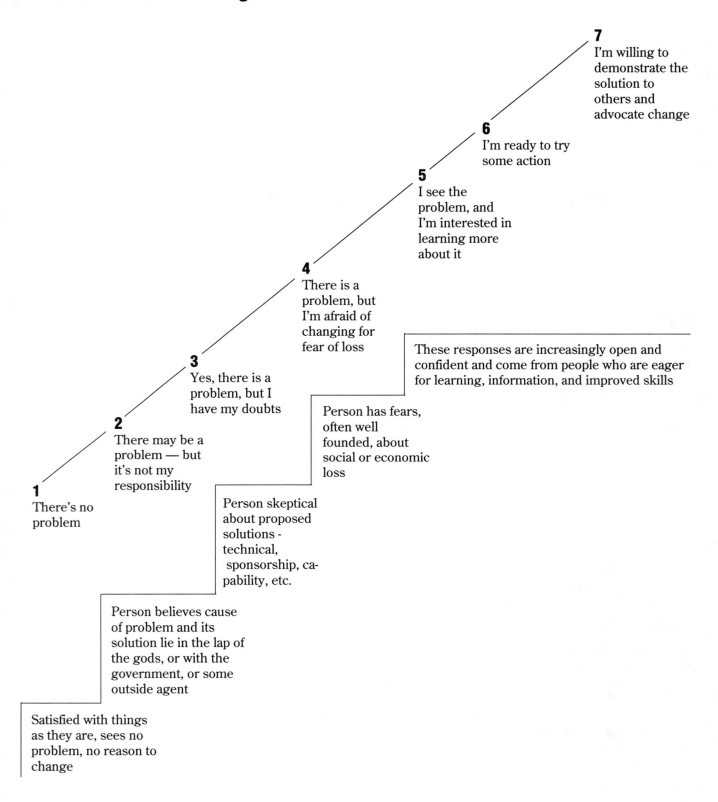

7
I'm willing to demonstrate the solution to others and advocate change

6
I'm ready to try some action

5
I see the problem, and I'm interested in learning more about it

4
There is a problem, but I'm afraid of changing for fear of loss

These responses are increasingly open and confident and come from people who are eager for learning, information, and improved skills

3
Yes, there is a problem, but I have my doubts

Person has fears, often well founded, about social or economic loss

2
There may be a problem — but it's not my responsibility

Person skeptical about proposed solutions - technical, sponsorship, capability, etc.

1
There's no problem

Person believes cause of problem and its solution lie in the lap of the gods, or with the government, or some outside agent

Satisfied with things as they are, sees no problem, no reason to change

NOTE TO TRAINER:

This activity goes to the core of the work of extension workers: how to understand and work with a range of local attitudes towards change. It should be given sufficient time so extension workers can deeply reflect on the learning.

Although there is no fixed order in which theoretical concepts are introduced, this exercise is generally scheduled early in the workshop since it helps to clarify the rationale for participatory approaches.

The RTCC is a simple, analytical framework for differentiating among attitudes towards change, by sorting them out along a scale showing varying degrees of resistance or openness. It shows diagrammatically the most resistant attitude on the extreme left where the individual does not recognise the existence of the problem at all, to the most open attitude on the extreme right where, in addition to adopting the change at a personal level, the individual is ready to advocate it to others.

Because of the difficulty of fine-tuning and categorising different types of resistant attitudes when taken out of context, the RTCC does not pretend to be anything more than a rough device for sorting out positions we commonly come across in our village work. What it does is to help us think about the relevance of different educational strategies in relation to this range of attitudes.

The inevitable conclusion is that one cannot use the same approach with people who are at stages 1 through 4 as with those at stages 5, 6 and 7. The latter would probably respond well to straightforward message-focused didactic materials since people at these stages are ready to accept and apply information. However, with people at stages 1 through 4, one would first need to draw out their own viewpoints and gain insight into the attitudinal constraints before attempting to convince them about a new idea. For this purpose, learner-centred materials would be more useful.

There are three methods that can be used in this exercise. Consider the time you have and the amount of participation you want when choosing a method.

After each of the methods, ask the group: "At which stage would people be most receptive to didactic teaching? Which kinds of strategies are more useful in the resistant stages? What value would participatory methods have for people at different points of the continuum?"

PROCEDURES:

■ Ask the group to cite some examples when they have observed resistance to an outsider's messages because of local beliefs, values and attitudes long sanctioned by traditions and culture.

■ Some examples given by participants in a PROWWESS workshop are:

   ■ Breast-feeding during pregnancy is harmful to a child due to drinking impure milk.

   ■ Eggs are not good for infants. They cause convulsions.

   ■ The uterus does not belong to a woman but to her husband.

   ■ Pregnant women should not eat watermelons. They cause too much water in the womb.

   ■ We don't want to cover our wells. The presence of frogs improves the taste of water.

- Flowing water is clean water.

- Mothers-in-law should not share a latrine with a son-in-law, or a father-in-law with a daughter-in-law.

- If you throw feces in the bush, whomever picks it up can harm you.

- Diarrhoea is caused by heat, especially in the summer.

■ Point out that often these beliefs are not openly expressed to an outsider but, until they are aired and discussed in a respectful way, they will not make room for an outsider's point of view.

■ Proceed with one of the three methods and the questions for the group.

Method One:

Distribute the balloon cut-outs to the group. Briefly explain the continuum diagram and ask participants to note if the balloon(s) they have received correspond to any of the stages of the continuum. Ask them to reflect on their balloon quotations but not to identify them with any of the stages until you have completed a description of all seven stages.

Method Two:

Show the poster and ask what the expected response of average villagers may be to the message contained in such a poster. In other words, they should react as villagers to the advice or message given in the poster. Have one or two members note down these responses on separate "thought balloons" as they are called out.

Next explain the continuum stages and ask group members to place their quotations along the different stages of the continuum. Their brainstorming should include the possible responses of average men and women in the village as well as of local leaders and those who have had some exposure to modern ideas (through army service, working in the mines abroad, etc.).

This type of brainstorming results in long lists of possible attitudes drawn from the participants' own experience from working with villagers or from what they have learnt from interaction with other extension staff. Thus you can relate the continuum to knowledge that is meaningful to the participants themselves and in which they have a personal investment.

Method Three:

Ask the participants to make up their own continuum based on the range of possible community responses, both positive and negative. To do this they will need to classify the community responses which they have identified into a continuum illustrating the degree of resistance or openness each represents. Have them consider what generic attitude underlies each of the specific responses they have identified. Does it reflect apathy? Lack of confidence in the feasibility of the idea? Denial that a problem exists at all? Fear of the social or economic risks of being an early adopter?

You must make sure that the gradations they illustrate are in a logical sequence of openness to change.

The RTCC was first published by World Education in "Workshop Ideas for Family Planning Educators".

Resistance to Change Continuum

Stage 1
Complete denial of the existence of the problem

Example: We have been drinking water from this river for generations. It never harms us.

Stage 2
Problem is recognised but the will to act is missing due to a feeling of powerlessness, apathy, dependence or fatalism.

Example: We need water but it is up to the government to build a water system for us.

Stage 3
While the problem is recognised, there are some doubts and fears inhibiting the adoption of the solution, such as:

Doubting the motives of the agency.

Example: They are only giving us a pump so that taxes can be raised.

Doubting the competency of the extension worker.

Example: What do these urban girls know about child care? They are not even married.

Doubting the community's readiness to cooperate.

Example: It won't work in this village. People are too lazy.

Doubting one's personal capacity to effect change.

Example: What can I do? I am only a woman. I have never been to school or I am too old, too poor.

Stage 4
There is some interest in the proposed change but also fear of the social, economic or other risks involved.

Example: I would like to have a latrine for the family. But what if my children still fall sick? The neighbours will laugh at me. They are against the idea of latrines.

Example: The local leader asks that we all contribute towards the costs of the pump's maintenance. But, what if it costs too much? I can't afford another debt.

Stage 5
There is real interest in learning more about the proposed change with a view to adopting it.

Example: There is a lot of bilharzia among boys in this village. Tell me how it can be avoided.

Stage 6
There is readiness to adopt the change.

Example: At night or when we are sick, a latrine is very convenient. I want to build one.

Stage 7
Not only is the new idea accepted and applied but there is readiness to convince others to adopt it as well.

Example: You can count on me. I will teach other mothers how to prepare an ORT solution for their children who have diarrhoea.

Example: I know how to fix and maintain the pump. I will be glad to show others so we can save on repairs.

Johari's Window

OPEN - Both parties know each other at least superficially and the relationship seems friendly.

BLIND - The outsider (extension agent) can see problems and their solutions clearly but the insider (villager) does not see them at all.

HIDDEN - The insider (villager) has certain feelings, beliefs, values, fears, etc. which only insiders are aware of. They are hidden from outsider's view.

UNKNOWN - Neither party knows the other well. They may however get to know each other better in the future in the course of working together over a period of time.

Fig. 2

JOHARI'S WINDOW

PURPOSE:

To facilitate communication between field workers and community members by creating greater awareness about degrees of inter-personal communication.

TIME: Under 30 minutes (1 hour if role play follows)

MATERIALS:

Johari's Window (SARAR adaptation) drawn on large size paper, and four separate labels (See fig. 2).

NOTE TO TRAINER:

This analytic model takes its name after its two authors, Joe Luft and Harry Ingham, both psychologists, who were concerned with different styles and processes of interpersonal communication. To illustrate differences in degrees to which two people may be mutually aware, they devised a model with four quadrants or WINDOWS labelled OPEN, BLIND, HIDDEN and UNKNOWN (see fig.1). The SARAR adaptation of this model includes pictures of two people facing each other at each Window with eyes open or blindfolded to represent the degree to which mutual understanding has been established (see fig. 2). The

	Known to self	Not known to self
Known to others	1 Open	2 Blind
Not known to others	3 Hidden	4 Unknown

Fig. 1

person shown inside each Window represents an average villager and the person on the outside represents the extension agent.

This tool helps participants realise that extension workers generally relate to the community from Window 2: They feel they have all the right answers to village problems while the villagers are considered to be ignorant or blind. Extension workers therefore may try to instruct the villagers, thereby hoping to help them open their eyes (overcome ignorance) and see things as clearly as the outsider does. The expectation is that villagers will then change their behaviour to match the outsider's instruction. This strategy has seldom proved effective.

The tool also brings home the point that the outsider (extension agent) facing Window 3 is in fact as good as blind when working with villagers without first getting to know their true feelings, beliefs, and values, which are not often disclosed by people until genuine trust has been established. This serves to remind participants that establishing trust, by listening to the people with respect and providing them with opportunities for self-expression, is the starting point for opening Window 3. This should have precedence over teaching people the outsider's agenda as in Window 2.

Finally, the most effective way of opening Window 4 is through a process of reciprocity and horizontal relationships with villagers by which the community's rich experience, knowledge of customs and beliefs, and intimate understanding of the local situation, can be integrated with the extension worker's technical know-how.

That this concept makes good sense to the participants is evident from the fact that once understood, they constantly refer to it. One team in Zimbabwe actually adopted it for use in their field work to sensitise the commercial farmer on the need to establish dialogue with his farm workers. In the attached adaptation, (fig. 3) the team also decided to exchange the places of Windows 1 and 4 so as to lead to a positive conclusion.

PROCEDURES:

■ Post a large Johari's Window (adapted) on the wall. Place the four labels on one side, in mixed up order: BLIND, UNKNOWN, OPEN, HIDDEN.

■ Give a brief explanation of the model as in Fig. 2. (Do not identify which label goes with which Window.)

■ Start with the explanation of the "Blind" Window, then the "Unknown", then the "Open" and last the "Hidden". Use minimum words as in the Note under Fig.2. Speak slowly so that participants can study the four Windows as you speak.

■ After explaining all four labels, invite a volunteer to come up and place the four labels on the windows. Check if all agree with the way they have been placed. If there is controversy over Windows 2 and 3, let all views be aired and then say why Window 2 is labelled "Blind" and Window 3 "Hidden".

■ Invite discussion of the relevance of Johari's window to extension workers contacts with villagers.

■ Time permitting, invite participants to role play the Windows.

Adaptation of Johari's Window (Zimbabwe)

Fig. 3

Theory

FORCE FIELD ANALYSIS

PURPOSE:

To help participants understand the theory behind the planning techniques they will use in their own planning and in adapted form at the village level.

TIME: 1 1/2 hour

MATERIALS:

Three copies of a large chart (approximately [1.5 m x .6 m] 5 ft. X 2 ft.) with the diagram below but without the labels.

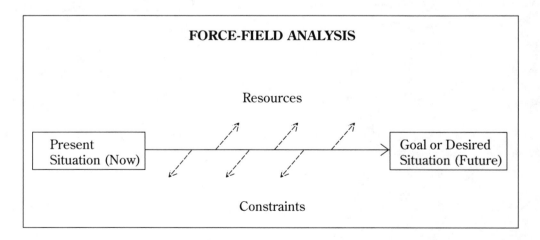

FORCE-FIELD ANALYSIS

The box on the left should have a picture of a problem situation, e.g. a woman carrying a heavy load of water.

NOTE TO TRAINER:

Trainers must know how to introduce planning concepts and skills at the community level in simple ways and also be able to apply such skills for themselves at a more complex level.

Once the group has done the "Story with a Gap" Activity (*Methods/Planning*), p. 118 participants will be able to relate more easily to its abstract form, as in the diagram above.

This exercise takes the group much further than the "Story with a Gap"; it requires, not only the identification of action steps, but also identification of the resources and constraints which affect the achievement of the desired goal.

It also helps to prepare trainers for their own major task of planning follow-on activities to use the participatory approach in their own work upon completion of the workshop.

For an example of how this theory can be presented in a more concrete form to village groups see the "Carts and Rocks" Activity (*Methods/Planning*), p. 121.

PROCEDURES:

■ Divide participants into 3 groups.

■ Post one of the three charts on the blackboard.

■ Explain the diagram and add labels as you go along, e.g. the box on the left represents a current situation (write *Now* above the box) which we hope to change. Ask the group what they consider to be wrong in the picture shown in the box. The other box on the extreme right represents an improved or ideal future situation, a goal to work towards in moving away from the present problem. (Write *Future* above second box and add a date to suggest a specific time frame for achieving the goal).

■ Point to the direction of the central arrow as you emphasise that the movement is away from the *now* towards the *future*. Explain that the arrows pointing towards the "Now" box represent constraints or forces holding us back from achieving our goal. While the arrows pointing towards the box on the right represent resources or helpful forces which aid us in moving forward. Add the labels *Constraints* and *Resources*.

■ Tell participants that each group will be given a copy of the chart. Their first task is to define in detail what is wrong in the *now* situation, then to spell out the desired *future* situation or goal, and then proceed to identify the *resources* and *constraints* which apply in that particular case.

■ Hand out all three charts.

■ When the groups have completed their tasks, invite them to report in plenary and open up a discussion based on the analysis done by the groups.

■ Explain the second task, which is to select any one constraint and identify the steps that could be taken to counteract or eliminate it with the help of one or more of the resources identified.

■ Have groups report back and discuss as before.

Adapted from Kurt Lewin's Forcefield Analysis.

Theory

TRANSACTIONAL ANALYSIS (TA)

PURPOSE:

To provide background theory on how extension workers could interact with villagers.

To create awareness of the need to establish an adult-to-adult relationship in working with villagers rather than to approach them in a critical or patronising way.

To clarify that a child-child relationship in working with adults is also appropriate at times since spontaneity and playfulness can add an important element of enjoyment to the learning process.

TIME: 45-60 minutes

MATERIALS:

Newsprint, markers, pencil and paper. Three pieces of paper with *Parent, Adult* or *Child* written on them. Fold to conceal the message. Large cutouts of people (e.g. Maxi-Flans) representing the three ego-states "Parent", "Adult", and "Child".

NOTE TO TRAINER:

The TA theory claims that in our day-to-day relationships with others, we function from one or other of three ego-states—*Parent, Adult*, and *Child*—which we have internalised since childhood. We have found this concept to be an excellent means of bringing home to participants the importance of engaging villagers in dialogue on an adult-to-adult level.

To do this, we have first to help participants analyse for themselves the difference between an adult-to-adult relationship and a parent-child relationship. They begin this analysis by brainstorming the behaviours usually attributed to a Parent, an Adult and a Child.

From long lists of behaviours that emerge from this brainstorming, participants are better able to sort out the roles of *a Critical Parent* compared to *a Nurturing Parent* or *a Playful Child*, compared to *a Rebellious Child*.

They then analyse the way some extension workers tend to relate to the community, and become aware of the danger of playing either a Critical or Nurturing Parent role, treating villagers as ignorant, dependent or difficult children. The need to establish a more mature adult relationship based on mutual respect thus becomes evident.

At the same time, participants realise that, on occasion, we all need to relax, have fun, and relate on a simpler level of unquestioning mutual acceptance. This is the type of child-child relationship which finds its expression in parlour games, songs, sports, group dynamics, and other entertainment. The importance of all these activities as part of a learning process becomes clearer to the group through the TA theory as well as by direct enjoyment of such activities at the workshop.

PROCEDURES:

■ Ask participants to divide themselves into three groups. Have each group pick one of the three pieces of folded paper on which the ego-states *Parent, Adult* or *Child* is written. This will determine their topic for the next step. Each group will work on only one of these three states.

■ Ask them to brainstorm the typical qualities and behaviours associated with the state of being a Parent, an Adult, or a Child. They should write their lists of attributes/ behaviours on newsprint and indicate the "state" (*Parent, Adult* or *Child*) as the heading. The list of qualities or behaviours should be written in the form of verbs, for example:

PARENT:	ADULT:	CHILD:
cares	reasons	cries
scolds	plans	plays
worries	negotiates	gives excuses
demands		

■ Have participants post their lists on the blackboard and invite their comments on the behaviours listed. They should feel free to add or change until all are in agreement.

■ Help them sort out the Parent list into two categories "Critical Parent" and "Nurturing (or Overprotective) Parent". Similarly they should sort out the Child behaviours into "Playful" and "Rebellious" child.

■ Use the flexi-flans, or maxi-flans, or other people cut-outs, to reinforce the image of the three states. Explain the theory of transactional analysis in terms of each person having internalised the three states and of communicating and functioning from one or more of these three ego states such as in the following diagram:

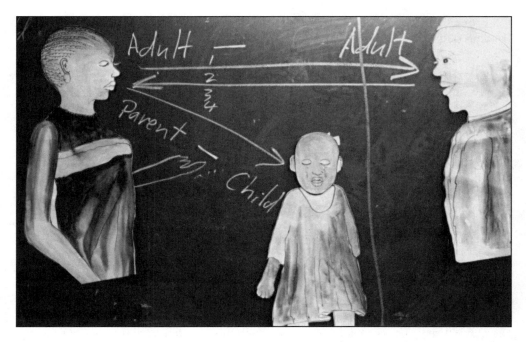

■ Explain that whatever state you communicate from (as in x above), it may condition the response of the other person. That person also may respond from any one of the three states.

■ Give concrete examples of how these types of transactions can take place within a family, in an agency or at the community level. Ask them to give examples from their own lives.

■ Ask them which type of role is usually played by extension workers in working with villagers.

■ Have them compare the insights gained from this activity with those gained from the "Johari's Window" Activity (*Theory*), page 167, if you have done that activity.

GLOSSARY

UNDP: United Nations Development Programme.

PROWWESS: Promotion of the Role of Women in Water and Environmental Sanitation Services. PROWWESS has been integrated into the UNDP-World Bank Water and Sanitation Program. It was formerly a programme of UNDP, which sponsored the workshops out of which this training manual evolved.

WSS: Water Supply and Sanitation Sector.

SARAR: The participatory training process described in this manual. The five characters signify (S)elf-Esteem, (A)ssociative Strengths, (R)esourcefulness, (A)ction Planning, and (R)esponsibility. See page 22 for further explanation of this approach developed by the author.

HARDWARE/SOFTWARE: These terms refer to personnel who deal with the technical and human aspects of WSS projects. HARDWARE refers to such staff as engineers and sanitarians; SOFTWARE to such staff as health educators and community development workers.

FIELD INSIGHTS: Examples, anecdotes, and report excerpts from real-life training applications and PROWWESS workshops. They provide a close-up view of how theory has been put into practice. These appear throughout the book to help illustrate content.

FOR FURTHER READING
AND TRAINING

CRONE, Catherine and Carman St. John HUNTER, Editors. *From the Field*, 1980. World Education, 210 Lincoln Avenue, Boston, MA 02111 (617) 482-9485

DEWEY, John. *Democracy and Education: An Introduction to the Philosophy of Education*, 1982. Darby, PA

FREIRE, Paulo. *Pedagogy of the Oppressed*, 1973. Harper & Row Publishers, Downsville Pike, Route 3, P.O. Box 20 B, Hagerstown, MD 21740, (301) 824-7300

HOPE, Ann and Sally TIMMEL. *Training for Transformation*, Vol. 1-3, 1984. Mambo Press, P.O. Box 779, Gweru, P.O. Box 66002, Kopje Harare, Zimbabwe, or Center of Concern, 3700 13th Street NE, Washington D.C. 20017, (202) 635-2757

INGALLS, John D., Editor. "A Trainers Guide to Andragogy", 1984. (Training Manual No. T0015), Peace Corps, Information Collection & Exchange (ICE), 1990 K Street NW, Washington, DC 20526, (800) 424-8580

KEEHN, Martha, Editor. *Bridging the Gap: A Participatory Approach to Health and Nutrition Education*, 1982. Save the Children, 54 Wilton Road, Westport, CT 06880, (203) 226-7271

KINDERVATTER, Suzanne. *Women Working Together for personal, economic and community development*, 1983. (Available in Spanish and French) OEF International Publications, 1815 H Street NW, Washington, DC 20006, (202) 466-3430

KINDERVATTER, Suzanne. "Learner-Centered Training for Learner-Centered Programs", 1977. Center for International Education, University of Massachusetts, 285 Hills South, Amherst, MA 01003, (413) 545-0465

KNOWLES, Malcolm, S. *The Modern Practice of Adult Education from Pedagogy to Andragogy*, 1988. Prentice Hall, Mailorder Sales Department, Old Tappen, NJ, (201) 767-5937

PFOHL, Jacob; Joshi Raju and Singh Manjuri. "Workshop: Education for Participation", 1984. Nepal: SSNCC

SRINIVASAN, Lyra. *Perspectives on Nonformal Adult Learning*, 1977. World Education, 210 Lincoln Street, Boston, MA 02111, (617) 482-9485

SRINIVASAN, Lyra and Sarah TIMPSON. "A Participatory Training Overview", 1987. UNDP/PROWESS, 12th Floor, 304 E. 45th Street, New York, NY 10017

VELLA, Jane K. *Learning to Listen*, 1985. Center for International Education, University of Massachusetts, 285 Hills South, Amherst, MA 01003, (413) 545-0465

VELLA, Jane K. *Learning to Teach*, 1989. OEF International, 1815 H Street NW, Washington, DC 20006, (202) 466-3430, or Save The Children, 54 Wilton Road, Westport, CT 06880, (203) 226-7271

PROWWESS/UNDP PUBLICATIONS: LESSONS, STRATEGIES, TOOLS

PROWWESS/UNDP Technical Series

As part of its mandate to replicate experiences, PROWWESS is developing, documenting and disseminating information on the participatory methods it promotes and on the outcome of their use. This can help to enrich policies and programmes, both nationally and internationally.

For this purpose, a Technical Series: "LESSONS - STRATEGIES - TOOLS" was launched in 1988 and includes:

LESSONS

case studies, research reports, evaluations, giving lessons from specific experience;

STRATEGIES

guidelines for project analysis, planning, monitoring and evaluation, strategies for inter-agency action;

TOOLS

field manuals and instruments for training in participatory methods, materials production, participatory research.

LESSONS - General

1. PROWWESS/UNDP: *Women, Water and Sanitation - or Counting Tomatoes Instead of Pumps,* by Siri Melchior, March 1989, (English/French), 22 pp. General overview of issues, lessons learned through PROWWESS.

   Also available as an introduction to a reference collection of basic documents on women, water and sanitation, available in full text on compact disk (ROM), "Library-to-go", by Decade Media with support from INSTRAW. To order this compact disk, contact Decade Media, Inc., 1123 Broadway, Suite 902, New York, N.Y. 10010, U.S.A.

2. International Reference Centre in collaboration with PROWWESS/UNDP: *Annual Current Literature Review on Women, Water, Sanitation.* Third issue forthcoming. Contact IRC, P.O. Box 93190, 2509 AD The Hague, The Netherlands for further information on subscriptions.

LESSONS - Case Studies, Country Reports, Field Research

3. UNDP/World Bank Water and Sanitation Programme and PROWWESS/UNDP: *Kenya - People, Pumps and Agencies*, by Deepa Narayan-Parker, August 1988, and South Coast Handpumps Project, Final Report, by L.K. Biwott. Companion reports on the South Coast Handpumps Project. One is a case study by PROWWESS analysing the role played by KWAHO (Kenya Water for Health Organisation) in partnership with Government and donors in community participation. The other report, by Government staff, is on the overall project evolution. To obtain, contact UNDP/World Bank Water and Sanitation Programme, 1818 H Street, N.W., Washington D.C. 20433, U.S.A., (English, 32 pp. and approximately 100 pp. respectively).

4. PROWWESS/UNDP: *Dhaka - Volunteers Against Diarrhoea*, by Elsie Shallon, December 1988, (English, 25 pp.). A description of a programme working with women volunteers in an urban slum area to improve health education and action, with limited technical inputs. Data on what health habits had effect on diarrhoeal rates, how changes occurred, level of participation and its role in implementation.

5. PROWWESS/UNDP: *Indonesia - Evaluating Community Management*, by Deepa Narayan-Parker, August 1989, (English, 39 pp.). A case study of PKK/Ministry of Health Activities in West Timor. Emphasis not only on changes occurring (effects on water use, maintenance, economic situations, women's lives) but particularly also on the framework for analysis, as well as the methods of data collection, particularly participatory research.

6. UNDP/World Bank Programme and PROWWESS/UNDP: *From Pilot to National Programme - Rural Sanitation in Lesotho*, by P. Evans, D. Narayan-Parker, R. Pollard, M. McNeill, and R. Boydell, 1990, (English, 26 pp.). Case study on evolution of a privatised rural latrine construction programme, including the role of community participation and health education. Includes data on costs and cost recovery, health effects.

7. World Health Organization and PROWWESS/UNDP: *Four research reports, Indonesia, Nepal, Sri Lanka, Thailand*, 1988 (English, each 100-200 pp.). The reports are the result of four studies of action projects which seek women's involvement in water and sanitation, showing participatory research methods utilised, the role of data in project implementation, as well as documenting the changes which occurred in the communities.

8. World Health Organization and PROWWESS/UNDP: *Final Review of Case Studies of Women's Participation in Community Water Supply and Sanitation*. Report of a Workshop held in Kupang, Indonesia, May 1988 (English 40 pp.). Discusses lessons learned from four reports mentioned under item 7 for such future research activities.

STRATEGIES - Guidelines for Project Planning, M&E, Inter-Agency Strategies

9. PROWWESS/UNDP: *PEGESUS* by Deepa Narayan-Parker, April 1989 (English/French/Spanish, 11 pp.). Analytical framework for designing and assessing projects and programmes, concentrating on goals and management tasks.

10. PROWWESS/UNDP: *Goals and Indicators for Integrated Water Supply and Sanitation Projects*, by Deepa Narayan-Parker, April 1989, (English/French/Spanish, 20 pp.). Indicators for planning and evaluation, within framework mentioned under item 9.

11. UNDP Central Evaluation Office: *Findings*, 1990, (English, 4 pp.). Short description of an evaluation framework for water/sanitation projects, based on items 9 and 10.

12. PROWWESS/UNDP and INSTRAW: *Interagency Task Force on Women - Proposals for 1989-90*, 1988, (English, 14 pp.). Reviews progress with respect to women's participation in UN organizations active in the water/sanitation decade, assesses major challenges for the future, proposes a work plan for agencies concerned.

TOOLS - Field Manuals, Training Instruments

13. PROWWESS/UNDP: *Tools for Community Participation*, by Lyra Srinivasan, 1990, (English, French, Spanish forthcoming). A field manual for trainers. Particular emphasis on SARAR methodologies, experiences in application in PROWWESS/UNDP activities.

Complementing the manual, a video is available (VHS, English in NTSC and PAL, French in NTSC and SECAM).

The above are available as a package from PACT, 777 U.N. Plaza, New York, N.Y. 10017, USA

Reports of training workshops which explain the methodologies in detail are available (a regional workshop in Burkina Faso, report dated April 1989, French, 26 pp. and annexes; A regional workshop in Tanzania, report dated February 1989, English, 31 pp. and annexes).

14. PROWWESS/UNDP *Field Manual on Participatory Research*, by Deepa Narayan-Parker (1993, English/French/Spanish). On the basis of about a dozen field research activities undertaken with PROWWESS assistance and within the framework of planning and indicators mentioned under items 9 and 10, this describes participatory research methods which have proven effective, how their role in planning, implementing and monitoring can be optimised, organisation of field research.

15. PROWWESS/Afrique and Banque africaine de développement: *Femmes et environnement : Méthodes et outils pour un développement durable*, 1992, (French, English forthcoming). A compilation of African experiences with participatory methods and tools for the planning and implementation of environmental projects.

Unless otherwise indicated, publications are available free of cost from PROWWESS.

For more information on PROWWESS programmes and publications contact:

PROWWESS
UNDP-World Bank Water and Sanitation Program, TWUWS
The World Bank
1818 H Street, N.W.
Washington, D.C. 20433, USA
Tel. 1 (202) 473-3994
Fax 1 (202) 477-0164